Praise for *Lead Like You Mean It*

⚜

"If you want to lead with integrity in your business and life, then you have to start with intention. Laysha Ward shows you how."

—Maria Shriver

"Insightful, timely, vital, and practical . . . Laysha Ward has her fingers on the pulse of what makes a great leader in the modern workplace. Ward is smart, rational, and savvy in her approach to meaning-based leadership to solve some of the greatest challenges we face, from isolation to burnout to disengagement."

—Shawn Achor, *New York Times* bestselling author of
The Happiness Advantage and *Big Potential*

"I've learned from Laysha for many years, and now she has provided everyone with a road map to leading with integrity and humanity in our lives and careers. Warm, resonant, and actionable, *Lead Like You Mean It* is an essential guide for anyone who wants to center themselves with purpose."   —Eva Longoria Bastón, actress, activist, and director

"The first principle of great leadership is to know what matters—to you. Laysha Ward's *Lead Like You Mean It* is an important primer on how to discover meaning in your life, and then bring it to your work as a leader."

—Arthur C. Brooks, Harvard professor and
#1 *New York Times* bestselling author

"In *Lead Like You Mean It*, Laysha provides an insightful guide on how to lead with integrity, humanity, and purpose, drawing on decades spent walking the walk. This candid, inspiring book is rich with leadership lessons that are both timeless and urgent. Highly recommended for anyone looking to build a meaningful career, drive business impact, and leave a lasting legacy."   —Brian Cornell, chair and CEO of Target

"Laysha Ward is a master at building meaningful, authentic relationships. From earning community support for Target's store openings to forging mutually beneficial partnerships at the highest levels of government, Laysha's work has empowered her to live her purpose of being in service to others. In *Lead Like You Mean It*, she draws on three decades of experience, from the department store sales floor to the Fortune 50 C-suite, to offer hard-won wisdom and practical advice."

—Thasunda Brown Duckett, president and CEO of TIAA

"Laysha Ward's stories in *Lead Like You Mean It* convey the strength that comes from powerful human connections and the grace that is bestowed by gratitude. Instead of sharing a formula for success, Ward shares what she has learned and encourages readers to participate, thoughtfully designing their own life and leadership-learning journeys."

—Walter Isaacson, historian, business leader, professor, and bestselling author

"Laysha Ward's trailblazing leadership example is an inspiration. But it's her humanity that teaches us the most. Laysha shows us what's possible while also living a life of purpose, intention, and fulfillment. Thank you, Laysha, for walking the talk!"

—Deborah Roberts, co-anchor of *20/20* and ABC News senior correspondent

"Self-belief has been a critical factor in my success. In *Lead Like You Mean It*, Laysha Ward illustrates the importance of knowing yourself and betting on yourself through her own life stories. Along the way, she shines a light on men and women who have influenced and supported her on her journey, delivering a beautiful tribute to authentic human connections."   —Serena Williams, twenty-three-time Grand Slam champion, investor, and entrepreneur

LEAD
LIKE YOU
MEAN IT

LEAD
LIKE YOU
MEAN IT

Lessons on Integrity and
Purpose from the C-Suite

Laysha Ward

THE OPEN FIELD / PENGUIN LIFE

Dear Reader,

Years ago, these words attributed to Rumi found a place in my heart:

> *Out beyond ideas of*
> *wrongdoing and rightdoing,*
> *there is a field. I'll meet you there.*

Ever since, I've cultivated an image of what I call "the Open Field"—a place out beyond fear and shame, beyond judgment, loneliness, and expectation. A place that hosts the reunion of all creation. It's the hope of my soul to find my way there—and whenever I hear an insight or a practice that helps me on the path, I love nothing more than to share it with others.

That's why I've created The Open Field. My hope is to publish books that honor the most unifying truth in human life: We are all seeking the same things. We're all seeking dignity. We're all seeking joy. We're all seeking love and acceptance, seeking to be seen, to be safe. And there is no competition for these things we seek—because they are not material goods; they are spiritual gifts!

We can all give each other these gifts if we share what we know—what has lifted us up and moved us forward. That is our duty to one another—to help each other toward acceptance, toward peace, toward happiness—and my promise to you is that the books published under this imprint will be maps to the Open Field, written by guides who know the path and want to share it.

Each title will offer insights, inspiration, and guidance for moving beyond the fears, the judgments, and the masks we all wear. And when we take off the masks, guess what? We will see that we are the opposite of what we thought—we are each other.

We are all on our way to the Open Field. We are all helping one another along the path. I'll meet you there.

Love, Maria

To my mother, Gloria Ward, and my late father, Gene Ward—
thank you for the roots of remarkable ancestry that flow though me.

To my husband, Bill Kiffmeyer, you are loved and love.

Contents

Introduction

I n the summer of 2002, I was asked to be one of the speakers at Target's National Sales Meeting as a last-minute replacement for my boss, who had a conflict. I had very little public speaking experience at the time and was way outside my comfort zone. OK, I was terrified. Yet I was also very excited to be asked to step up. The invitation was an incredible honor, and it was a major opportunity to talk to the Target team and our partners about our meaningful work.

I'd come a long way from the young woman who started her career with the company on the sales floor at Marshall Field's in Chicago. I was now a director, overseeing all of Target's community relations and the Target Foundation. My job involved bringing business and communities together and ensuring that Target had a positive impact on the communities we were in. It was work I cherished, and I was excited to spread the word.

Yet here I was being asked to speak, alongside our seniormost leaders, in front of ten thousand of my fellow team members and our partners! Knowing I'd need to project the kind of energy necessary to address the corporate equivalent of a sold-out concert was intimidating enough. To top it off, as one of the very few people of color in mid-management, I felt an added burden to represent all people of color.

The invite had plunged me deep in the throes of imposter syndrome. Who was I to offer my thoughts to such an experienced group? I wanted a career with meaning, one where I created real impact and led change. However, my fear and anxiety weren't telegraphing that this was the opportunity to do just that; they were telling me I was in over my head.

Thankfully, I had a mentor in none other than Mrs. Coretta Scott King. I'd met Mrs. King the year before during a collaboration between Target and The King Center, and after the successful completion of the project, she graciously agreed to be one of my advisors. Beyond her stature as the wife and legacy holder of Dr. Martin Luther King Jr.'s dream, she had dreams of her own, and I valued the wisdom that she generously shared with me. I even appreciated her challenges, such as the times when she would firmly put me in check with a stern look, saying, "Now, Ms. Ward . . ."

Mrs. King accepted my invitation to speak as a guest during my presentation at the meeting. And as we stood together backstage, I could have put on a brave face for her (and Lord knows I wanted to!). Instead, I confessed, "I've never spoken in front of this many people. I'm afraid." This woman of extraordinary courage, wisdom, and grace laid her hand on my arm, looked me in the eye, and said, "Laysha, you have earned the right to be here. Do what you have to do. Do what you have been called to do."

It was just the reminder I needed to stand confidently and bring my voice to the work I was so passionate about and so honored to share. As I stood on the stage in my for-good-luck red power suit, Mrs. King's affirmations gave me the strength I needed to claim the opportunity I was ready for. They gave me the strength to remember my purpose: that I was blessed to have work through which I could share my gifts and create opportunities for so many others—that I was blessed to be able to lead with meaning.

♠

When I first began this book, I was still executive vice president and chief external engagement officer at Target. My thirty-two years at Target and my position where I was both part of the leadership team within—focusing on business strategy—and consistently working with the community and external leaders in government, business, community groups, and more, gave me a unique vantage point on purpose and leading with meaning.

I've also been able to follow my passion for connecting people within the community and outside of it through my service on for-profit and nonprofit boards, and by volunteering with nonprofits and civic organizations. I mentor, sponsor, and serve as an ally for others, both inside and outside of work, helping people be the best versions of themselves. I also have close friends, family, and found family that I love, and who complete the circle of meaning in my life.

In other words, I've seen and participated in the quest to lead with meaning from all sides. I bring that distinctive perspective to this book. I was leading with meaning that day of the National Sales Meeting and am always trying to lead with meaning now.

What do I mean when I say "lead with meaning"?

In its simplest sense, it's exactly what it sounds like: It's working and living with integrity and humanity. It's having impact. We want financial security, we want a personal life, and we want meaningful work. We want to make a difference. We want to find a way to "do what we've been called to do," as Mrs. King advised. We don't want to lose our values and, in pursuit of financial security and career success, get sucked into a dead-end job. We want a life filled with purpose and to leave behind a meaningful legacy.

How do we do all these things, especially in today's divisive times? We are often made to feel like what we want is impossible. There have been books on how to win friends and influence people, how to think and grow rich, and how to lean in, but we have no clear guide on how to lead a successful life and career that's purposeful and intentional.

Let me assure you, however, there is a way. It isn't perfect. But it's an important step in the right direction. It's what I call leading with meaning. And it's a pathway to achieving all of the above. Leading with meaning entails viewing your life and career as part of the same puzzle, acting from your purpose, making intentional choices, nurturing relationships, and championing and sustaining yourself and others. When you lead with meaning, you are taking a holistic approach that blends your life and career. You are part of something that's bigger than yourself, staying aligned with your purpose no matter what life throws at you or how your purpose evolves. You are stepping into, rather than shying away from, new relationships, even with people from completely different backgrounds. And you are committing to bettering yourself and others. When you're leading like you mean it, you are shaping a legacy that leaves people and things better off than you found them. You are living a life in which you're giving more than you're taking.

To be clear up front, this is not a book on work-life balance. I don't believe in work-life balance per se. I believe in a holistic approach to your life and career over time. This approach asks you to make intentional choices. For example, sometimes you need to decide: Are you going to the big job interview or are you going to your best friend's wedding? This isn't balance, it's being aware that our choices prioritize different aspects of our life and work over time, and even in a single day or moment. When you are mindful in your choices, you can create a joyful and purposeful life for yourself alongside a successful and meaningful career. Not always easily. But it is doable and you're worth it.

I also want to clarify that even though I use the word "lead," it doesn't mean that this is only a book for those already on the leadership track. You can lead with meaning through your actions at any stage of your career. As I always say, do what you can, with what you've got, from where you are. Whether you're an assistant or a CEO, if you act with integrity and humanity and take a holistic approach, you're serving as a role model and an example to others. You're also setting the tone and template for a life well lived, a set of principles that you can continue as you advance in your career.

Now, let's manage our expectations for a minute about leading with meaning in our careers. There may be limits to how much you can lead with meaning at work. You do have choice and you do have power. But it is not realistic to expect that our jobs can be all things to us. There are limitations to what companies can do. Companies must make profits and they have a responsibility to multiple stakeholders: They must answer to their customers, their community, their team, and their shareholders. And not all those groups want the same thing. Companies have to balance very different interests with their business strategy.

Leading with meaning starts with knowing your purpose. Your purpose is your rock. It is the base against which all else must be measured. It is what you must return to again and again, especially when you have lost your way. Your purpose connects you to your core values and helps you ground yourself in the impact you want to make. (I'll help you begin to identify your purpose in chapter 2.) If you're truly leading with meaning, your purpose will always include, at least in part, a desire to be of service. This doesn't mean you can't also want to make money. As I'll explain further, I think good business and meaningful impact go hand in hand.

Another key to leading with meaning is building and maintaining nurturing relationships. Successful leaders do not operate in a vacuum; they engage the outside world and draw power from their connectedness. Your authentic relationships buoy you, and shine a light when the road appears dark, as Mrs. King did for me. Relationships inspire you to stay connected to your purpose, help you get clear on your goals, and support you in finding solutions. And no, I'm not just talking about connecting to the powerful or a civil rights icon. Your key connections might be with your hairdresser, your spouse, your real estate broker, your peers, or with a junior—or senior—colleague. Without the wide range of relationships I've forged, and the allyships I've benefited from, I never would have had the career I've had. And by turning toward rather than away from the world, I've been able to unlock opportunities and meaning I never could have envisioned creating for myself—or others.

A third essential piece of leading with meaning is the sustaining of self and others. Having been the recipient of so much guidance and wisdom from so many stellar individuals has helped me develop an understanding of leadership that's focused on others' growth and potential. In contrast with older, more authoritarian styles, this is a management style that emphasizes coaching, care, sponsorship, and advocacy. Women and people of color have often been overmentored and undersponsored. What I'm advocating for in leading with meaning goes beyond that. Sustaining others means championing their impact, lifting them up, and propelling them forward through active sponsorship. And not forgetting that we must sustain ourselves as we do so.

Purpose, relationships, and the sustaining of self and others—these are the linchpins of leading with meaning. And they all require not only inner knowledge, but outward engagement.

In my case, all three got me to the C-suite and helped keep me there. Throughout, I have learned to own and refine my personal style—which I think of as "C-suite meets street-suite." And in case you're thinking, "Well, that will never be me," here's the thing: When I was young, I never would have imagined the life of service and leadership I've been able to forge.

I grew up in a town in rural Indiana with a population of just seven hundred people. I began my educational journey in Head Start, an early education program for low-income children and families. I was the only Black student in my class from first grade through senior year. Obviously not the most likely path to the C-suite in corporate America. I was petrified the first time I walked into my first-grade classroom without a single friend, and terrified to open my mouth knowing the other students would soon discover that I had a lisp and couldn't pronounce words the way they could. So, trust me, little Laysha is just as surprised as you are that those humble beginnings led her to a ride of more than thirty years up the corporate ladder and around the world, visiting every continent. All of which helped me lead with a blend of confidence and humility. What I can say with certainty: Staying rooted in my purpose, the relationships I've built, and sustaining myself and others has been critical to my success and my journey.

⚶

When I sat down to finally fulfill this years-long dream of writing a book and passing on to others what I've learned, I discovered something interesting: The advice that younger folks were asking me for and the advice my own mentors had passed down to me was remarkably similar. Perhaps I was ahead of my time, or perhaps I was just lucky, but impact and change have always been at the core of my life and career path. And with the guidance of many other wise women, including Mrs. King, and men, I've been able to lead with meaning. In a corporate environment, no less—and outside of it.

In this book, I will show you how to do the same. In the following pages, I'll share the lessons I've learned along the way, to provide a series of stepping stones for you as you work toward leading with meaning. My hope is that these lessons will be as life-changing for you as they were for me. That they will help you transform your life and leadership journey. And that they will help ground you in your purpose, help you become a leader who lives a truly connected life, and help you lift up others, transforming yourself and everyone around you for the better.

Part 1 of this book will focus on the first steps to creating a more holistic life and career: investing in you. In chapter 1, we start with betting on and believing in yourself: how to know yourself, show yourself, and take care of yourself. Before you lead others, you must first do the work on yourself. Chapter 2 discusses how to figure out your purpose or "why," the crucial rock that you will return to again and again to figure out the path forward.

Part 2 looks at how we build and maintain relationships, as I believe that in work and life we get better together. In chapter 3, I take you on a tour of how I've engaged with wider communities as part of my goal of being of service, and how you too can find meaning through that type of engagement. In chapter 4, I help you begin to build your "kitchen cabinet" and develop a portfolio of connections to level up your connection currency.

Part 3 identifies specific tools of a leadership practice that puts meaning into action and enables us to work well and live well. In chapter 5, I encourage you to move forward to growth, to step outside your comfort zone and get uncomfortable, because where there's discomfort, opportunity is not far behind. Chapter 6 discusses effective communication: As you learn to listen and listen to learn, engage in healthy debate, and negotiate, you will be better equipped to create solutions that solve a problem and add meaning at work and in the world. And in chapter 7 we look at processes that empower people, foster collaboration, and drive results.

Part 4 discusses how to sustain yourself and others as we maintain our holistic approach to a life and career grounded in humanity and integrity. In chapter 8, I'll show you how to develop a thriving team and culture by nurturing the values of care+, learning, and trust. And in chapter 9, because leaders are people too, we'll examine the importance of creating space for our personal relationships and flourishing together.

In a final Benediction, we'll pause for a moment to consider the impact of an intentionally connected life.

Throughout, I combine advice on how to work on yourself, with advice on how to develop your leadership skills and impact. I believe these things are inseparable. Balancing all aspects of well-being, while navigating the highs and lows of life and career, is the key to a well-lived life.

Building a life and career rich with purpose and relationships, one that sustains you and others, is not simple. It takes discipline, fortitude, and vulnerability. Our world is facing unprecedented challenges, from macroeconomic shifts, geopolitics, supply chain challenges, and labor shortages to the evolving future of work and political polarization—not to mention the many, often conflicting perspectives on how to address these issues. Leading with meaning is a full-contact participatory sport that will require you to get off the sidelines and into the game in a way that will stretch you and even surprise you.

In these pages, I will often ask you to be open and vulnerable. It takes vulnerability to know who you are, put yourself out in the world, and know that you are worthy and belong in any and every space you enter. In return, I will be open and vulnerable with you. It's the only way for us to truly relate. I will also be asking you to take small, actionable steps with every chapter. In return, you will discover new ways to create and live out a culture of connection, community, and meaning wherever you are, at any and every stage in your life.

Let's get started.

PART ONE

INVEST
IN YOU

CHAPTER ONE

Bet On You

*Tension is who you think you should
be, relaxation is who you are.*

—CHINESE PROVERB

L eading with meaning starts with you. You are where the journey begins and ends.

You are also one person. Personal *and* professional development are important at every stage of your life and career. We are whole human beings and everything I offer in this book starts from that basic truth.

You may be more accustomed to receiving advice on one realm or the other. Guidance on our professional side is often focused strictly on career development. In our personal lives, we may receive counsel on personal growth and relationships. There is often a wall between these spheres of advice. My advice is to take the wall down. You bring your full self to your life and career. Both personal and career development are an essential part of how you lead, and especially how you lead with meaning. When you act from your purpose, you make intentional choices to sustain yourself and others.

So how do we take a bet on our full selves? For some, this kind of self-belief is easy. Maybe you have no trouble being your own cheer-leader. But for those of us who come from places or spaces where we aren't accustomed to being the powerful ones, the journey to embrace our full potential, our full self, often requires preliminary work.

Here's a simple question I often ask people I coach and mentor: Do you believe in yourself?

It seems like an obvious answer—yes! But you'd be surprised at how many people stumble over it.

I get it. I've had my moments of imposter syndrome and fear, just like anyone else. As discussed in the introduction, I've stood on stages I wasn't sure I had the right to stand on and had to lift my head high and speak up. I know what it's like to fear that I'm not up to task. Fear is a natural response to learning new things or being put in unfamiliar situations. When it comes to the unknown, fear is perfectly normal. We've all been there.

Some of us also carry an extra burden. You might fear you don't belong because you have imposter syndrome. But you also might be afraid because you've been told, either overtly or in so many words, that you don't belong, that you aren't worthy. Roger Ross Williams's 2023 documentary, *Stamped from the Beginning*, based on the book by Ibram X. Kendi, discusses how every Black woman has had her Phillis Wheatley moment when, often under interrogation, she feels compelled to "defend her worth." Finding your confidence and belief in yourself is never easy. It's infinitely harder when you've encountered that kind of doubt from others just by virtue of who you are.

Which is why I'd like to say to you up front what Mrs. Coretta Scott King said to me: Do what you have to do. Do what you are called to do. You have earned the right to be here. I believe in you.

What you also must know is that you can and will learn to move through the situations that provoke fear and anxiety. Nelson Mandela said that courage was not the absence of fear, but the triumph over it. When you've moved through fear once, you'll gain the confidence to keep moving through it. Again and again. Until that tingle of anxiety becomes an old friend. And the feeling of having triumphed over the fear becomes as familiar, if not more familiar, than the fear itself. You will learn to do new things. Things others may have never thought you capable of. You may even excel at them. It can feel hard initially, but you will always move through it. Because you believe in yourself.

If you believe in yourself, others are more likely to believe in you too. If you don't, they won't. Unfortunately, it's often that simple. But that simplicity also gives you great power. Your belief will lead the way for everyone to see you as you truly are: capable, powerful, and magnificent.

Remember, you don't need to know everything up front—or ever. We continue to grow and learn. Rest assured: You will do something great at every stage. You are exactly where you need to be. I believe in you. Believe in yourself.

Who better to take a bet on than you?

Know Yourself, Show Yourself, Take Care of Yourself

To make a winning bet on yourself, you must know yourself, show yourself, and take care of yourself. These are the fundamentals to master before you can lead others. They will also make it easier for you to lead with meaning, as a continued practice of knowing your-self, showing yourself, and taking care of yourself reinforces and con-tinually surfaces what is truly meaningful to you.

Learning to figure out holistically who you are and what you want is valuable at every stage of your life and career, whether you're a se-nior executive or just starting out on your journey. You are the CEO of your life and career, and at different stages we face different kinds of challenges, both personally and professionally. You get to choose where you want to focus your attention at any moment, any day, and over time.

You're always evolving and thus continuously being asked to fig-ure out who you are. Getting your first apartment, starting a family, becoming an empty nester, taking care of an aging parent: All these things ask us to redefine ourselves and require balancing your per-sonal and professional development. These changes in your personal life also affect who you are and what you want to impact, which is key to leading with meaning.

Let's not forget that rapid evolution on the professional side also affects who we are and what we want to impact. Business and the world are constantly changing. As we keep up with that rapid pace and evolve our skills accordingly, or even pivot in our careers to try something new, we may be presented with novel opportunities. For example, if artificial intelligence (AI) technologies come into your field, you may no longer need to spend time on written summaries for others. AI can do that for you. Yet those same technologies may also give you an opportunity to do more creative and strategic work, which may connect you to a different set of colleagues. That, in turn, could change your vision for how you can lead with meaning.

Being grounded in who you are and the meaning you want to make, no matter what stage you are at or how the world changes, is a competitive advantage. And when I say competitive advantage, I'm not talking in terms of a company's advantage, I'm talking about setting yourself up for success and betting on yourself, your whole self.

In today's fast-paced business environment, you will have to reinvest in yourself over and over again throughout your life and career span. When I left Target after thirty-two years, I had to put this theory into practice. Even as I continued my volunteer nonprofit work and my company board service, my day-to-day work was no longer with a Fortune 50 company behind me. Now it was Laysha-the-start-up creating a website, writing a book, developing a new portfolio for my life. I had to take a bet on me, all over again.

As much as you change, you are always you. Remember, the world needs the original you, not an imitation of someone else. I'm sure you've already heard the mantras: Be yourself, be authentic. What you don't hear, however, is that authenticity isn't something you get from the outside and wrap yourself in. And authenticity isn't something you create. Authenticity is something that's already there, deep within you. It's in your roots.

Know Yourself (and Spin Your Roots into Gold)

For a long time, I resisted telling people where I was from. I didn't feel comfortable sharing that I was raised in small-town Indiana. I didn't want people to know that I had long been an "other"—the little Black girl with afro puffs, the only Black girl in the class from first grade to twelfth grade, who "talked funny" because she had a lisp. I didn't want to be seen as a country bumpkin. I was embarrassed to tell my colleagues that, yes, I'd plucked a chicken and milked a cow. I didn't want them to know I came from a place where "farm to table" wasn't a trend, it was how we lived; at our dining table we literally ate food we'd picked ourselves. Now I can fully appreciate it, but early in my career, I actively avoided the subject of my roots.

When I did begin to talk about my background, however, I found people welcomed learning more about me. They appreciated my vulnerability in sharing who I really was. They saw the strength and resilience that I learned at an early age, growing up in rural Indiana, as invaluable assets. And by sharing, I began to see myself and my roots as positive too.

Which was a valuable lesson. Because it turns out that many of the very same attributes that you see as your curse growing up are your superpowers. Those things you dismiss or hide as part of your less than glamorous past? They are often unique assets that can help you succeed. You just need to flip the picture. And spin your roots into gold.

One note of clarification: I'm not trying to minimize the difficulties of growing up working poor or anything else. I very much appreciate the challenges folks face, including those who have had real trauma in their background. My point is simply that part of accepting and believing in yourself, especially when you're young, is learning that you aren't defined by the most negative interpretations of yourself and your backstory. And that if you can open yourself up to more positive alternate interpretations of your past or your attributes, you may discover all kinds of riches.

When I began to reframe my roots into something more positive, much to my surprise, I realized that being from a rural background offered significant advantages for my work at Target. It turned out that growing up poor, in a rural environment, with parents who held down multiple jobs to give my siblings and me a good start in life, was a valuable asset in my ability to connect with a wide range of consumers and employees. This connection to our customers gave me a unique point of view and insight into our business practices. For example, precisely because I'd had an intimate connection to food growing up, I was able to understand and ask questions about Target's entry into the grocery business in ways that benefited the company.

When I was young, we lived on ten acres of land. To offset our limited means, we picked wild greens from the field (yes, I've filled trash bags full of greens, collard and otherwise!) and ate vegetables straight out of our huge garden. So when Target ventured into fresh food, I was very interested in where our greens were coming from, in which stores we were offering them, and how affordable they would be for *all* guests (the term Target uses for its customers). Colleagues joked about my obsession with greens, but my childhood connection to fresh food came forward in my work. While my role in Target's food strategy was infinitesimal compared to those who led and implemented the strategy, I am proud that Target became a place where consumers could get fresh, quality produce, including greens, at an affordable price.

It was an interesting circle: The more I owned my background, the more I realized I could use it in ways that benefited the business. My discovery, in turn, of my connection to our customers fueled my work. Remember what I said about how knowing yourself *enables* you to lead with meaning? This was that in action.

My upbringing also helped me connect to those in our community who couldn't afford plentiful spreads on their table. There are a lot of people in both rural and urban environments who don't have enough food. When I was young, we'd always can and freeze vegetables from our garden to carry us through the winter season. And, no surprise, in a small rural environment, we shared our stockpiled food with others in need. Growing up in a community where hunger was prevalent gave me an early understanding of these issues. And decades later, leading Target's corporate social responsibility efforts gave me firsthand understanding of hunger issues in the communities where Target operated. My personal experience also gave me helpful perspective when it came to Target's support of and participation in a hunger relief strategy and its initiatives, including a large food donation program. It was inspiring for me to see team members across the organization bring this commitment to life over time.

Again and again, insights from my rural upbringing have helped me lead in ways that benefited my company and the larger community. Being true to myself and my past helped me see what others wanted and needed and what would benefit communities that weren't being served. The attributes I initially wanted to hide have turned out to be important drivers in my service to others. I was a low-income kid who went to Head Start. I don't think it's an accident that I ended up leading a billion-dollar community education program for Target that was aligned with the top priority identified by our guests at that time.

I'm not alone in finding gold in my roots. Temple Grandin, an autistic animal scientist, used her insights into the therapeutic nature of deep embraces to develop a calming "hug machine" for cattle and a "weighted blanket" for humans. She came across the idea of a hug machine on a relative's farm. She also knew from personal experience that deep pressure stimulation alleviated her own symptoms of autism.

Marie Van Brittan Brown invented an early security system that used a camera that could slide into the four peepholes in her door and transmit the images to a monitor. It was 1966 and Marie lived in Queens, New York. When her husband was away, she didn't feel particularly secure; she knew from long experience that the police weren't all that reliable at responding in her neighborhood, which she'd lived in her whole life. Marie had no formal schooling in engineering, but she and her husband patented her invention, and it became the baseline for future home security systems.

You can also spin your roots into gold in more personal ways.

The gold in my roots has been instrumental to my own particular style, which I call "C-suite meets street-suite." It's about keeping it real and relatable, from the break room to the boardroom. I can burst into a gospel song with the best of them, and I can do a mean breakdown of a balance sheet.

C-suite meets street-suite also describes my fashion sense. When I was in college, like many students, I couldn't afford the latest shoes or trendiest fashions. So I learned to get creative with clothes. I quickly discovered that I didn't need a large budget; anyone can create a sense of style with what they've got. I would pull together pieces from thrift stores and secondhand stores to reflect a flair and a look that was uniquely mine. Vintage clothes were my swag. They were how I was able to express my style. And to this day I still love checking out secondhand pieces. I almost always rock something from Target at a black-tie event—or find something from a thrift store. And I'm OK with that! Doing just as much with less isn't a negative to me anymore. It's a positive. Finding a great deal is one of my superpowers. And I love it.

Knowing yourself is a lifelong journey. As you learn more about yourself, you will keep peeling back the layers of growth as you become more comfortable showing the world who you are. You will find gold in your roots, and in standing strong in the person you're discovering—and revealing to others. No matter what stage you're at, every time you discover something about yourself you become more proficient and effective at doing what you were meant to do and making an impact in your chosen profession.

> • What are some unique experiences that you had in your childhood?
>
> • Even, or maybe especially if, you view those experiences as negatives, how might you reframe them as a positive?
>
> • What's an attribute of yours that you might have seen as a curse growing up but that, if reframed, might be your superpower?
>
> • How can you spin your roots into gold?

Show Yourself (and Stand in Your Power)

Part of betting on yourself is learning to show yourself. You cannot assume that others will understand where you are coming from. And you cannot leave it to other people to write your story, because they will write that story based on how they want to see you, rather than who you are.

You must tell your story and tell it clearly.

I know it can feel uncomfortable. I was raised to be humble and not sound like I was bragging. Early on in my career, this was a tension that I often faced. Do I speak up? Or just swallow my version, put my head down, and get on with what I'm doing? I was also in a company where there is no "I" in team and we were all encouraged, for many years, to stay out of the spotlight. Everything was in service of the team—not a single individual.

The problem is that if you aren't sharing your story or helping others see the impact of your work, sometimes your bosses will see it anyway, but sometimes they won't. You may get lucky and find a boss willing to take the time to help pull your story out of you, but many will be too busy or distracted with other things.

I advise the people I mentor to write up their own performance reviews in advance. This is something I always do as well. It's a way of documenting what I've accomplished in a given period. I'm not waiting for my boss to say what I did. I become the author of my own narrative. My pre-review isn't just me shouting my accomplishments. I call out what I've done already and what I've yet to do. By taking the lead on the evaluation, I exercise self-awareness and clearly convey my performance and my potential to my boss. Note: The point isn't to block the feedback others give you, but rather to articulate for yourself and others the goals you're committed to and your progress toward them. You're listening to others and you're showing yourself. Who better to sketch the initial outlines of your work self-portrait than you?

Showing yourself also means learning to stand up for yourself and to stand in your power. Betting on yourself means believing in yourself—and not letting others bully you. I know this will be hard for some of you to hear, but we all have to learn to advocate for ourselves. Putting your head down and doing the work isn't sufficient. You have to advocate for yourself and share your story in a way that puts *your* narrative out in the world.

Now, honestly, this is something I've struggled with my entire life and career. I continue to struggle with it. I haven't always done this perfectly. I'm still a work in progress. But I have learned a great deal from those who have mentored me, including Bob Ulrich, a Target CEO, who taught me to stand in my power.

As CEO, Bob Ulrich transformed Target into an upscale, fashion-forward discounter that attracted a more affluent clientele than our early discount competitors. He is a legend in retail, known for his laser-sharp focus on the company's brand, strategy, and team. During his tenure as CEO, he utilized his impeccable eye for good design. He cared deeply about the details and influenced everything—yet he never micromanaged his leaders, and instead taught us all to be stewards of the "bullseye."

Bob was known for wearing jeans and cowboy boots (including a bright red pair for major company meetings), smoking cigarettes, drinking Coors Light, and having zero patience for any form of bullshit. If the word "gruff" had an image in the dictionary, it would be a photo of Bob. He mumbled, cursed, and critiqued, but we all knew that, at his core, there was a compassionate heart and a relentless drive to deliver for our guests, team members, shareholders, and communities.

Bob never sought the spotlight, preferring instead to give his team recognition, and he disdained celebrity CEOs. He knew the power of relationships and connections for our business, but he didn't want to be the one to do it. He wasn't hung up on hierarchy either. He was confident in his own leadership and expected the rest of us to lead with confidence too. He never blocked me from having connections with founding members of the company, including Mr. Bruce Dayton, who I grew close to. Bob was generous with connections like that.

Hierarchy was out when it came to determining which leaders would attend important forums too. So I often found myself in places that even my boss had never been—like serving on board committees, or roundtables at the White House, or being Target's representative for the Library of Congress's National Book Festival, working closely with then First Lady Laura Bush for eight years in the early aughts. While it was daunting, repeatedly being at events with world leaders and influencers gave me exposure that bolstered my confidence as a leader.

In the moments when I felt that Bob was beating up on me at the

Target "family table," I reminded myself that he was doing it to prepare me to succeed at the global table. And he was hard on everybody,
not just me. He continually pushed us to rise to the occasion—or
break under the pressure (which some did). Fortunately, if a bit stub-
bornly at times, I rose to the occasion. Yet we had differences of opinion that sometimes led to tense moments—and to my realization that
I could, and sometimes should, stand in my power.

Once, on a business trip with Bob and other senior leaders, I was
late for the company jet departure. Well, I wasn't exactly *late*. "Late"
in Target vernacular meant "later than Bob." Our goal was always to
beat Bob to the jet hangar. It was one of those unwritten rules that
you figure out with time and experience. In this particular case, I was
later than Bob—but right on time by the itinerary.

As I walked onto the plane, Bob was sitting in his usual seat near
the front, holding a newspaper in front of his face. Without moving
the newspaper, he said, in an irritated tone, "Next time you're late,
we'll leave you behind." And without thinking, I said, in a similar
tone, in front of everyone on the jet, "Well then, next time, leave me."
I had just committed a Target cardinal sin by allegedly being late to
the jet. And then I doubled down with sass.

The flight back was icy.

What I don't regret about that day is that I stood up for myself.
From Bob's perspective I was late because I had arrived after he did.
But I had been on time by our flight plan. I had been meeting with
the governor's office and the First Lady of the state we were visiting
and following the schedule. Unbeknownst to me, Bob wrapped up
his own meeting earlier than expected. But my "lateness" (which was
really on time) was justified.

But I unpacked it in my mind after the trip. I recognized that I
could have—and should have—done better. Delivering a snarky

reply was beneath me, and I knew it. Part of standing in your power is speaking your truth. It is also thinking through your responses. You always want to consider:

- **Message:** What you want to say.

- **Audience:** What you know about who you are speaking to that might influence the conversation.

- **Vehicle:** The forum or channel where you'll be communicating.

- **Timing:** When you will communicate.

- **Tone:** The voice you will use to deliver the message.

The order in which you do this is less important than that you think through each element to design and deliver the message that best reflects your narrative.

Here's what I should have done to stand in my power: I could have listened to Bob, then immediately (Timing) calmly (Tone) responded to Bob (Audience) that I *was* on time and that I had had a successful meeting (Message.) And left it at that. I should have responded immediately in person (Vehicle), which I did. But I should have gotten my story out clearly and calmly, which I clearly did not. I could have articulated my response—I'd been at a successful meeting and I wasn't late—and spoken up for myself. I don't know that Bob would have been any less grumpy in the moment about waiting for me. But ultimately, he always respected me standing up for myself.

If people call you out, you have to learn to find your courage, your power to speak your truth. It's important to find the diplomatic way of doing so, but making yourself seen, heard, and respected is a key skill in leading with meaning. Advocating for yourself and sharing your story as you want it to be shared is a crucial element to betting on yourself—and getting others to bet on you.

* Think about a time you wish you'd stood up for yourself.

* What could you have said or done to "stand in your power"?

* How could you have used Message, Audience, Vehicle, Timing, and Tone to frame the narrative and show yourself?

* The more you practice telling your story, even in retrospect, the more it will come naturally to you.

Take Care of Yourself (and Know What You Need in the Moment)

None of us leads or plays at 100 percent all the time. Even when you're leading with meaning, things will happen outside of work that may profoundly affect you and your ability to do your job. That's OK. What you do need to be able to do is to connect with yourself—and *know what you need in the moment.* You can't lead with meaning if you're falling apart. This is basic self-care. It also sounds a lot simpler than it is.

Many of us were taught that there is no emotion in the workplace. This was often reinforced with a message that we have a work self and a personal self, between which there needs to be a barrier. But any barrier of that sort is artificial. I can be objective and still bring emotion to a situation. Objectivity and feeling are not mutually exclusive. In fact, giving yourself permission to feel and be empathetic is *how* we lead with meaning—we bring our humanity to everything we do.

It can be particularly hard for Black and brown women to give themselves permission to feel. That's because—and I speak from lived experience—we believe we don't have time to break down. For many Black people, we don't want to give over our emotions and our vulnerabilities because we don't always know how the people who are in the presence of that vulnerability are going to use it.

Right after George Floyd's murder, I was preparing for a keynote address at a women's college. The world was going through an intense racial reckoning, and I was living in the epicenter, at ground zero, in Minneapolis. We were also in the middle of a full-blown pandemic. I was juggling a lot and trying desperately not to drop the glass balls that would shatter versus the rubber ones that would bounce back.

I remember being on a Zoom call with the team and someone asked me, "Laysha, how are you doing?" I had grown accustomed to responding to that question by saying I was fine and moving on. But that day, without warning, I started sobbing. I had to turn off my camera and put myself on mute. Within a few minutes, I was able to get myself together and come back on camera, but I was clearly not fine.

While I both preach and believe that it's OK not to be OK, as a part of my own healing journey, I had to determine when, how, and with whom I shared my emotions. During that time, to keep myself on track, I picked up a little trick of standing in front of my mirror each morning and asking myself, "How are you feeling?" I started wondering if I was losing it as I practiced my response in front of the mirror every single day. But I knew it was necessary for me because I was struggling. Sometimes my response back to myself in the mirror allowed me to feel centered and ready to move through the day, and other times I bawled uncontrollably.

Throughout this difficult chapter, my boss Brian Cornell, CEO of Target, checked in on my well-being—repeatedly. He reminded me, in no uncertain terms, that I wasn't Superwoman. He pointed out that if I didn't take care of myself, I wouldn't be any good for the others I deeply wanted to help. He wanted me to avoid burning out and to have the stamina and endurance to deliver on my purpose at this critical time. I was telling others to take care of themselves, but I wasn't taking care of myself—a walking, talking classic case of "Do as I say, not as I do." Brian was empathetic and understanding. He also saw what I needed and wasn't acknowledging for myself: I needed to take some time for self-care. Because if I didn't deal with my pain, my pain would deal with me.

There's an old saying that "Black don't crack." But the reality is, it may not crack on the outside, but it does on the inside. I desperately needed to take off my strong, resilient Black woman cape and trade it in for much-needed rest. Brian helped me see this by holding up the mirror and showing me that I needed to get better at knowing my needs and acknowledging them to others.

This experience allowed me to dispel the myth of the strong Black woman. While we are strong, we are also human.

There's a larger lesson in here for all of us about acknowledging our humanity and needing to look at our life and career more *holistically* than we generally do. We are all vulnerable to falling apart at moments of extreme pressure or personal challenge. We are all human. And what happens in our life affects our career and vice versa.

Throughout this book I emphasize looking at your total well-being. By total, I'm referring to your physical, mental, spiritual, social, and financial health. Knowing what you need in the moment is also part of this comprehensive view: We are people who think, we are people who feel, and we are people who do. Practicing any kind of self-care, including in the moment, is essential. It's how we refill our cup.

Here's some personal recovery tips for when you're feeling unduly stressed:

Take a moment. Step back and ask yourself what you need in the moment. Do you need to keep moving through it? Or do you need a moment to process?

Breathe. In times of difficulty and emotion, it's always important to remember to breathe. When you feel yourself starting to struggle, pause, then take three long, deep breaths. This is a tip I got from my beloved speech coach, Teresa Lyons-Hegdahl, and it has always stayed with me. In and out, in and out, in and out. Deep and slow. This will help calm your nervous system.

Think through your options. What are your immediate needs and what kind of space or boundaries might you require? Perhaps you're on a Zoom or in a meeting with colleagues when you receive some deeply affecting news. Do you need to take the day off? Put the issue in a box if you can't pause right away and set aside some time to think on it later? Leave the meeting completely? If you're on Zoom, maybe it's good enough to just turn off your camera? What are the rules for your engagement in this moment or in the next moment? Only you know what you need.

Acknowledge the demands on you. When there is a lot going on, it's OK to just go ahead and accept the pressure. Call the moment what it is. Acknowledge what is being asked of you. Don't run from it or toward it. Just sit with it for a moment.

Determine what you need. Set aside some time to think about your longer-term needs. If it's helpful (clue: It often is helpful!) talk through those needs with others. What do you need today? Next week? Next month? Make a list of what you need help with. Remember, what you need and what someone else needs are not necessarily the same. And that's OK. What's key is to gain the self-awareness of your own needs and acknowledge them to yourself and others. That is doing the work.

Give yourself permission to say what your needs are so people know. Others need to know what works for you. I know it can be awkward to have these conversations, but you must tell your boss and your coworkers what you need. If you aren't open about your needs, others can't help you meet them. And if you are open, you might be surprised how willing others are to help. After all, they are betting on you too.

Know that it's OK to have needs at any level, in any role. We all have things that make us feel othered or alone. It doesn't matter whether you are entry-level or the CEO. Every human will have times when their needs interfere with their work. Expressing those times when you need support or acceptance, whether you're dealing with historical events or an aging parent, can give other people the courage to share their needs.

Ask for help. Believing in yourself does not mean doing it all. Thinking that you have to do everything yourself isn't betting on yourself, it's a sure road to burnout. You must be vulnerable and ask for help when you need it. What kind of help you are looking for goes back to your needs. Perhaps you're a working parent who needs to locate kind, supportive, consistent childcare to free you up to get your work done. Perhaps you need a trainer or even exercise buddy to help you maintain your exercise routine and your mental health. Perhaps you need to speak with a therapist. Perhaps you need a wonderful stylist like Ms. Ruby, an incredible woman in North Minneapolis who does my hair and so much more, about whom I will have much more to say later. The point is you need to surround yourself with others who can and will assist you. No one does everything by themselves. You don't need to bear your burdens on your own. Help is available when you are courageous and willing to ask.

⚜

Remember: Basic self-care helps you help yourself and help others. It's not weakness, it's strength. Never neglect your total well-being. You can't take care of others if you don't take of yourself. You want to be able to run the full race; you want to be resilient. You need the stamina and fortitude to stay the course.

Any self-aware leader will address both their personal and their professional needs. But if you're leading with meaning, this is especially important. You've made a commitment to bettering yourself and others. And you can't encourage others to take care of themselves if you're not doing it for yourself.

Being strategic about how we spend our time helps to ensure we can lead with meaning. How we take care of ourselves matters. Here are some suggestions on how to incorporate mental, spiritual, social, and physical health goals into your life.

- Prioritize daily gratitude journaling or a weekly time for your faith.

- Set a goal for the hours you will work and which hours will be designated as sacred time for yourself or your family.

- Establish guidelines for how often you're saying yes to social invitations.

- Set aside time for physical exercise and/or going to the gym each week.

Leading with meaning all starts when you bet to win. When you know yourself, show yourself, and take care of yourself. When you take a bet on you.

Next, we'll discuss how to find your why or purpose.

PS from Laysha

No matter what stage of your life and leadership journey you're in, believe in you. Claim your agency, manifest your dreams, and help others along the way. Your future self will thank you for the bet you take on yourself today.

CHAPTER TWO

Find Your Lunch Counter

Success is making ourselves useful in the world,
valuable to society, helping in lifting the level
of humanity, so conducting ourselves that when
we go, the world will be somewhat better of
our having lived the brief span of our lives.

—GEORGE DRAPER DAYTON

I could fill a book with the lessons Mrs. Coretta Scott King taught me over the years, including how to authentically live and lead by staying grounded in who I am and what I believe. But one conversation we had early on will never, ever leave me. It shocked me into action. And it ignited my purpose in a way that's kept the flame lit for the rest of my life.

I first met Mrs. King in 2001. At the time, I was in my early thirties and evaluating whether corporate America was the right place for me to fulfill my purpose and be of service. I was living in the Twin Cities, which, especially in that era, was not a very racially diverse place. And as I looked around my workplace, I saw very few people of color and only one Black person in the most senior leadership positions.

I wanted to have business impact and I wanted to have community impact. I wanted to be part of our business growth strategy, which included where we built and sustained stores. It was good for the business to serve different consumer segments; it was also good for the community. I also wanted to make sure I was able to advance in a way that would allow me to have even more influence in those decisions that impacted the community. I was ambitious.

But here's the thing: Sometimes you have to see it to believe it. And with no Black female leaders already in place, becoming one felt like a bit of a pipe dream. It was discouraging and hard to be on my own, and I was seriously considering moving into the nonprofit or government sector, where there would be more people who looked like me and whose ambitions like mine were to serve. There, at least, perhaps I could make a difference.

I decided to ask Mrs. King's advice. Her response was both immediate—and unexpected.

She said, "Laysha, corporate America is *your* lunch counter and I need you to sit there for a while. Not forever, but long enough to make a difference."

Corporate America was my lunch counter?

Initially, I was speechless.

This was not what I was expecting to hear. I understood her reference to the sit-in at Woolworth's lunch counter in Greensboro, North Carolina, one of the tipping points of the nationwide civil rights movement in 1960, eight years before I was born. I was, after all, talking to one of the true legends of civil rights. But she was imploring me to stick with my *business* career and follow my purpose there. Was she serious?

However, the more I thought about it, the more I saw her point. I had made a faulty assumption, early on, that leading with meaning meant a career of service in the government or nonprofit sector. I say faulty because I could already see in portions of my work and what I saw the company doing that there was potential to lead with meaning in my work too. Not in the activism sense, but in the sense of following *my* purpose. Finding my lunch counter wasn't literal; it was a metaphor for finding the right path to be of service and have impact. Leading with meaning can take many forms.

Sticking with the company wasn't what I initially wanted to hear. I still had the problem of feeling lonely there. But it was what I *needed* to hear. Mrs. King's words—her call to action to follow *my* purpose— set me on a path that transformed my life and career. Her point was that I didn't have to leave the system to improve the system. Instead, my presence in a Fortune 50 company would help create better results for the company and society as a whole. I would be making a difference for our guests, team members, shareholders, and communities. I even might become one of the too few people of color who found their way into senior management in corporate America (at the time, I wasn't even dreaming of the C-suite), work that could create a route for others to benefit. This, she was saying, is what I'd been called to do. I had a unique place at a table that she didn't. I enjoyed being in business. I was motivated to learn and grow while helping others do the same. And I was also starting to see that when done well, growth for the business also meant growth for our team—and for our communities, including communities that had long been underserved.

She also admitted it might be slow going. Now, when you are in your early thirties, hearing that you are signing up for slow-going change, change that you might not even see in your own lifetime, is a bitter pill to swallow. But she was right. Fulfilling your purpose isn't something that happens overnight. It takes time and it may involve a long period of discomfort. But if your passion for the change is strong, you will see that there is an arc to the progress. You will see the joy amidst the struggle. You will learn to be patiently impatient. And to push for the change you want to see, some of which may happen more quickly, some of which may not. Taking action is doing the work. Retaining your hope and commitment is paramount. This is working toward progress.

By imploring me to see that I could play a crucial role in opening the door to corporate America for underrepresented communities, Mrs. King helped me clarify my calling and my purpose. I wanted to be of service to others, especially women and people of color, and I wanted to open the doors to others. She made it crystal clear: I could do all that in business. I could do all that at Target while also contributing to the company's purpose, values, culture, and strategy.

Although I certainly didn't imagine it on that day with Mrs. King, ten years later I was promoted into the C-suite. And in total, I spent more than thirty years at that corporate lunch counter, doing the work and paying it forward. In my time at Target, we grew from $9 billion in annual revenue and fewer than five hundred stores to more than $100 billion and nearly two thousand stores, many of which were in new markets or markets that weren't previously served—representing significant growth in local tax revenue, community investment, volunteerism, and, of course, local hires. Change may be slow, but it does come.

Mrs. King helped me clarify how I could become the person I was meant to be. She helped me see my true purpose. A purpose of service that lay in an unexpected arena. But an arena that ended up being a perfect fit for me. I want to help you find yours. Wherever it lies.

Know Your Why

My purpose is to be of service to others. I serve to lead and lead to serve. It's something I've done since my earliest days when I volunteered for Special Olympics in high school. I continued to serve in my work at Target, my work on nonprofit boards, and my work on for-profit boards. Your purpose may differ. But if you want to lead with meaning, service will always be a crucial part of your purpose too. When you're leading with meaning, you're uplifting others and leaving people and things better off than you found them. Similarly, being of service is about helping people be the best of version of themselves, fulfill their potential, and have a positive impact in the community and world. Whether your purpose is to build and grow a small business, improve the environment, or represent your community on your school board, there will always be a service component if you're leading with meaning.

To lead a life of meaning you need to know your central purpose. Leading with meaning is leading with *your* purpose. Not someone else's purpose—not your employer's purpose, not even your mentor's purpose—but *your* purpose. Your purpose is more than a job or a title. It is something that resonates with you that transcends any specific career or track. Your purpose is the rock that you will always return to. It is the filter that allows you to make decisions about your life and your career. Whenever you stand at a crossroads, your purpose will be your guide.

Now, I know that purpose is one of those words that everyone bandies around. And many don't really know what it means or how it applies to them. Don't despair. I'm going to walk you through this. The key to articulating your purpose is specificity and, you guessed it, self-knowledge.

I suggest that as you work through the following set of questions, *write your answers down*. Written purpose statements, whether for organizations or individuals, drive meaningful results. They help you take a set of amorphous, abstract goals for your life and turn them into actionable measures. A written purpose is a lantern and a measuring stick all at once.

Finding your purpose starts with knowing your why. Here's a few questions to start:

- What do you want?
- Why do you want what you want?
- What impact do you want to make?
- How does that desired impact align with the organizations or places where you want to spend your time, energy, and talent?

Your answers to these questions and more will help you figure out what's meaningful to you and thus what you aspire to lead yourself and others toward.

To inspire you, let's look at a few examples of how the pros do it. Purpose statements are an organization's "why"—their reason for existing in the world. Both for-profits and nonprofits have purpose statements. For example, Target's statement of purpose is: "To help all families discover the joy of everyday life." Dove's is: "To make a positive experience of beauty accessible to all women." The mission of St. Jude Children's Research Hospital is to "advance cures, and means of prevention, for pediatric catastrophic diseases through research and treatment."

The first thing that might strike you is how different all the statements are. That's no accident. Every organization's purpose statement, like every organization, is tailored to its unique reason for being. We wouldn't confuse Target with Dove, or either Target or Dove with St. Jude Children's Research Hospital. Yet all three are broad enough to encompass a range of goals, jobs, and positions.

This combination of specificity with range is your goal too. You are not like anyone else. Your statement of purpose must be unique to you. It should not be so detailed that there is no room to grow. But it must be just detailed enough to reflect the special person you are and the unique journey you will take in the world. Let's dig deeper.

There are three elements to every great purpose. The first is the thing you're called to do. The second is the impact you want to make. And the third is some sense of the actions you will take to fulfill your purpose.

What Are You Called to Do?

A calling is something you feel uniquely pulled to do that's connected to desires you have and skills you have or want to develop. Consider what gives you energy. Think about the times you've felt fulfilled or proud. What were you doing in those moments? Your calling often lies in the things you do that light you up and that you instinctively offer others.

In our example, Target's calling is to foster the discovery of joy. That may sound strange to say about a corporation, but if you enter a Target store, you'll see the truth in the statement. From its bright red signage to its fun selection of items, Target is meant to be a joyful shopping experience. Dove's very different calling is to make a positive experience of beauty accessible to all women. As anyone who has seen the Dove campaigns knows, from their use of plus-size models to their self-esteem project, they have worked hard to redefine beauty, especially for vulnerable teens and women of all shapes, colors, and sizes. St. Jude's calling is to advance cures and means of prevention, and to treat children with cancer and other catastrophic diseases. They are passionate about finding cures and saving lives.

The corporate purpose statements are remarkably personal, and you too might find your calling in "fostering the discovery of joy for others" or "advancing cures through research or treatment." Here are some other callings to consider as you ponder your own. The chefs I know love creating beautiful and nourishing food and derive their purpose watching others delight in consuming it. My cousin loved fixing up cars and found his calling in seeing others able to benefit from his handiwork. I also have family and friends who have found their calling in protecting and serving, in problem-solving using cutting-edge technology, or in nurturing others and bringing love, whether as parents, educators, or in the caretaking professions.

OK, now you try. What's your calling?

Who Do You Want to Impact?

The next step is to think about who you want to impact. Do you want to be of service to a certain group? For example, do you want to help the next generation of talent at your organization? Small business owners? Your church community? The aged? The ill? The underserved? What groups or types of people do you feel a connection with? Is your purpose workplace- or community-based, or do you want to impact the world? Perhaps you want to protect the environment. Or foster art and culture. Or even support animal rescue.

The impact group identified in Target's purpose statement is "all families." Dove has many initiatives with different targets, from their teen self-esteem campaign to one for men on positive masculinity. St. Jude's focus is on helping children and families.

I have a friend who found their purpose in helping "other entrepreneurs." A finance expert I know helps advance financial literacy for those who have no background or exposure to financial affairs. A lawyer friend volunteers with an organization to help youth in her community with mental health issues. An accountant helps do the books for a group that helps veterans. The impact category you identify can be as broad or as specific as you desire. Whatever feels right for you.

What Impact Are You Trying to Make?

Knowing what you want to avoid and what you want to achieve takes thought. Don't worry if you need to take some time to really reflect on this one. Again, the more specific you are about the impact you want to have, the easier it will be to achieve your goals.

While we don't want to put words in anyone's mouth, here are some potential ways our organizations might perceive their impact. Target might view their impact in their guests' discovery of the joy of everyday life and in the surprises, fun, ease, and inspiration families experience at every turn. Dove's impact might lie in helping those who have not previously seen themselves as attractive appreciate their true beauty. St. Jude might see their impact in extending the lives of the children they treat, in their success in finding cures, and because their cancer research leads to breakthroughs that are shared with doctors and researchers globally, in the saving of thousands more children worldwide for every child saved at St. Jude.

Here are some examples from an informal survey of friends and colleagues. Remember the woman who wanted to help entrepreneurs? More specifically, the impact she wants to have lies in connecting entrepreneurs to opportunity, thus improving the entrepreneurs' lives and the lives of the people in the communities they support. Another executive wants to raise the next generation of Hispanic and African American marketing executives, thus supporting the men and women he feels a kinship with. A college graduate I know, working in her first professional job, wants to have an impact on pollution and climate change, even if it's just a quarter of a percentage point of progress.

Hopefully, by now you see how reflecting on your goals and drilling down to a reasonable level of specificity will help you take the next step: which is figuring out how to actualize them.

How Will You Do It?

The final question to ask yourself is, how will you do it? Think about the concrete actions you can take to really do what you're called to do. You may already be doing some of them. What new actions (big or small) can you take to bring your purpose to life? Write them down.

It's fine if some actions are conceived of more broadly, while others are more specific. Dove's calling is to create a more inclusive vision of beauty. They answer the "how" question specifically, saying they will achieve that goal by dismantling existing beauty standards. Their campaigns are aimed at doing exactly that—for example, forcing us to question why we assume only a narrow category of women are considered beautiful.

Perhaps your calling is to bring joy. Your "how" is that every week you intend to do something to surprise and delight your colleagues, family members, friends, or relatives. Your statement might be exactly that. Or your "how" might get very specific, such as whether you intend to spend time every week with the elderly or mentoring young adults. Our entrepreneurial friend's how is through offering "coaching, training, technical expertise, and giving others access to capital and markets."

Remember, the "how" is up to you and will adjust as you change and grow. As long as you are clear on your calling and specific about who you want to help, what impact you want to make, and how you will follow through, my bet is that you will find an endless number of ways to fulfill your purpose. And will have the time of your life doing so.

Make It Memorable

A statement of purpose can be as fun as you want it to be. Ideally, it's also memorable or sticky. Give it a whirl: How can you make your purpose statement clear, concise, and something you can remember? What would bring a smile to your and others' faces? How fun if your sense of purpose gives you, and others, a dopamine hit, a sense of joy or creativity. When it comes to corporate, I have a soft spot for Mondelez International's "Empowering people to snack right." You just know someone at that company has a sense of humor.

What's your unique angle? Perhaps you can come up with some language that reflects your unique style of connecting or resonating.

Or perhaps there's a special turn of phrase that reflects your personality. And don't forget to include the element that brings you joy. In the Mondelez example, I'd say the key "joy" element is snack!

The more effectively you convey your unique angle, your special twist, and your joy, the stickier your statement will be. And the stickier you make your statement of purpose (and yes, it's hard work, all good things are) the more memorable it will be for others—and you'll enjoy returning to it again and again.

As you create a personal statement of purpose, here again are the five key questions to ask yourself:

- What are you called to do?
- Who are you trying to impact?
- What impact do you want to make?
- How will you do it?
- What words could make your statement unique or memorable?

Here are some examples of personal purpose statements that combine all the different elements.

"My calling or purpose in life is to improve people's lives through entrepreneurship (*what, impact*). I want to do that for our employees, our customers, and our community (*who*). My company, Pinnacle's, purpose is to 'connect people with opportunity' (*how, words*)."   —NINA

"My purpose is to help people and the planet (*what, who*) through my job and my daily personal actions to conserve and organize others (*how*). I want to feel as if I've made the world a better place, even by a quarter of a percentage point of progress (*words, impact*).   —LAYNA

Now you try. What's your personal statement of purpose?

Align Your Purpose

Once you know your purpose or why, you're on your way to living a life that's centered around it. The next step is to figure out ways to align your purpose with your organization's purpose. For example, if you know that your calling is to connect, perhaps you want to get involved with one of your company's ERGs (employee resource groups) or volunteerism. If your calling is to teach, but you're working in a corporation, maybe you can offer to help train the new employees in your group area.

Aligning your purpose with your company or organization is what Maryam Kouchaki, professor at Northwestern University's Kellogg School of Management, and Isaac Smith, professor at Brigham Young University's Marriott School of Business, call "purpose congruence." With purpose congruence, you make the company's purpose your own, and you're able to shape how you weave it into your daily tasks and integrate it with your own purpose statement. If your company doesn't already offer you this option, ask. Most employers want their employees to feel motivated and to thrive via purpose congruence. If your workplace is open to these kinds of conversations, show your calling (remember, always be showing yourself!) and try to work the actions that motivate you into your daily life at work.

If you are at the stage of your career where you have a bit more autonomy at work and/or if you are at a turning point and are lucky enough to have multiple job opportunities to consider, here are three things to look for in determining whether an opportunity aligns with your purpose:

- Does the organization's purpose—and its people—give you a positive feeling? Will you be proud to be associated with this organization and fully support it—even if others don't see its value? This is the real litmus test. If you know deep down that a role or organization is right for you, even when others close to you don't share your passion or perhaps don't even support your choice, that's purpose at work.

- You'll also want to look for any synergies or points of intersection between the organization's purpose and your own. At the very least you want to make sure that your purpose and the organization's purpose aren't at odds with each other.

- Finally, you'll want to learn whether there will be opportunities to fulfill your personal purpose as part of your work. If the role gives you agency in how you fulfill your duties, fantastic. If not, will there be alternate ways to bring your purpose to life?

Keep in mind, there are few situations where there is perfect and total alignment between personal and organizational purpose. It's possible—but rare—and shouldn't necessarily be the goal.

It's worth asking yourself whether you believe enough in the organization's purpose to be fulfilled by your work. If there's a divergence between company purpose and your own, you might still find enough compatibility in the organization's culture and values to make the work meaningful for you. Or you might not. This is what you want to determine before you commit to working there. It's rarely about perfect alignment. But sometimes just enough is enough.

Stay Open at the Crossroads

Staying in alignment with our purpose can feel tricky because our jobs and careers do not stand still. Neither does our purpose. Over time, our purpose evolves and expands because our worldview and experiences evolve. It's also important to stay open and know that there is strategic serendipity: Things may not happen when you want them, but they are always right on time, right?

Sometimes you will feel yourself at a crossroads. You've evolved and you're no longer sure you and your job are aligned. Your purpose and your company's purpose may even be going in opposite directions. Then you have to make a decision: Do you stay or do you go? I opened this chapter with one such "crossroads moment" in my life. In that case, Mrs. Coretta Scott King came to my rescue and helped me clarify that I was still in alignment with my why. But there have been other turning points when I had to question my alignment with my company's. There are also times when you have to stay open to the unexpected route.

Very early on in my career, when I worked on the sales floor of Marshall Field's department store in Chicago, I assumed it was just a temporary job. I'd been thrust into business for the first time in my life. I was sleeping in my friend's closet in a small apartment, and I was excited to have some cash to pay for drinks at happy hour, because that's where we ate most of our meals. It was typical post-college life. At the time I did not have a stated purpose or plan, but I knew I wanted to be of service and make the world better. And at that age, it seemed obvious: Retail is not a place where people try to make the lives of other people or the planet better. My plan was to go into the Peace Corps. I wanted to make an early commitment to service and apply it in ways that might be useful globally or domestically, possibly leading to a nonprofit-sector job. The gig at the department store was just a pass-through. It was never the long-term plan to stay.

Which is where the strategic serendipity came in. I was waiting on my Peace Corps assignment when I got my first job at Marshall Field's. But as the weeks went by, working at the store, the more I felt intrigued by the business I'd joined. I loved that retail is consumer-facing. One of the attractions of the Peace Corps is that it has some social science research work in it. You're learning about people and cultures and you're looking to problem-solve the challenges other people face. At the end of the day, you're looking for very human solutions to human problems. Well, there I was in downtown Chicago interacting with lots of very interesting humans. Not just Chicagoans, but people who were coming in from all over the globe to shop at our store. Now, remember I had grown up in a town of seven hundred people. At that point I still had not even been on an airplane. My worldview was so tiny. And that worldview was getting expanded daily just by my interactions at the store.

I was further intrigued as I learned more about the Dayton-Hudson Corporation, now called Target, which had just bought Marshall Field's. I watched a video at work that was narrated by the woman who would become my boss, Kassie Davis, the head of community relations for the company. In the video they were talking about the company's history and community engagement and how important it was for the company to be involved in the community. They talked about the history of the Dayton family, a family who had a deeply rooted commitment to charitable giving, community investment, and doing well by doing good. And I remember thinking, "This is all so counter to what I thought companies could and would do." I was in uncharted territory.

My path was supposed to be going outside of the United States, into the Peace Corps, where I would learn a ton, and then eventually bring that learning back to the States, where I would apply it either here or in the Foreign Service. This was the first time it dawned on me: A U.S. market-based company *could do well while doing good.* Not only that, but a capitalistic company could have a commitment to social responsibility and impact. After all, companies could and did impact the lives of their consumers—and the lives of their team members.

I was blown away. I continued to bombard the store director at the time, John C., with questions. Soon, he gave me a volunteer and community engagement handbook, and I became the community captain for that store. Through this additional assignment, I learned even more about the business—and about how the store could get involved at the hyper-local level. I learned about all the things that the store could do, whether it was through making grants or volunteerism and in-kind donations.

In the meantime, I was getting good at the core parts of the business. I was crushing my sales goals and continuing to ask questions about the strategy of the company. I remember the day John C. told me, "You might have a career here. You're good at this. You should think about where this could take you."

I told him, "I can't do what you do."

I wasn't even sure I wanted to do what he did. But as I talked with him about what the store director role was, my worldview about impact shifted. Here he was leading a multimillion-dollar business with about five hundred employees and he was shaping people's lives. He was meeting with the mayor and connecting the business with the community. Suddenly I realized: There were things he was doing, that he and other business leaders did, that I did not have a clue about. I was completely ignorant—and had so much more to learn.

That's when it became apparent to me: I didn't have to go to the Peace Corps to serve people. I could make a difference in my community. Business could be a way to serve. And business could be a part of a solution to the problems I wanted to help solve. It struck me like a thunderbolt. This thing I was railing against was actually a hidden tool in the arsenal.

So I pivoted. And I didn't go into the Peace Corps. Instead, I moved from sales leader to department manager so that I could learn the business on a deeper level. And by learning the business, I was preparing to excel at the community relations role that I knew I eventually wanted to be in.

By staying in Chicago, my worldview expanded in ways I didn't expect. But my "why" stayed in place. My why was to be of service. It was the road to being of service, or to achieve my why, that ended up being very different than I had planned. And I had to be open to this new direction. The extraordinary opportunity to learn and grow and have impact was right there in Chicago.

Defining your purpose and aligning and then realigning your purpose is a continually evolving task. We all grow and change; our purpose often grows and changes with us. But knowing your why, reexamining it, and using it as your filter is an exercise that will keep you on track in your life and career. It will allow you to always lead with meaning.

> Tips for making your purpose real:
>
> * Name it and claim it. Share your purpose with others. Make it part of your story. Don't just say it, do it. Move your purpose "from the walls to the halls" through both your actions and your behaviors. Be clear about the steps you will take to live out your purpose through your daily routines.
> * Monitor progress and reset as you grow. Pressure test your purpose throughout your life and leadership learning journey and make changes as you change.

PS from Laysha

When you don't know where you want to go, you can end up anywhere, or end up somewhere you don't want to be, following someone's else's path, not your own. Purpose is power, but only when activated by action. Be curious and open. This will help you figure out what's meaningful to you and start taking the steps that allow you to lead yourself and others toward that life of impact.

PART TWO

GET BETTER
TOGETHER

CHAPTER THREE

Find Meaning Through Engagement

If your dream only includes you, it's too small.

—AVA DUVERNAY

I held many positions that I enjoyed at Target over the course of my thirty-two years there, and I loved them all, even when they were challenging. But I feel especially fortunate to have become a director of community relations as quickly as I did, as it was instrumental in shaping how I thought about leadership.

Here's what I discovered: Outward engagement is fundamental to leading with meaning.

As discussed in part 1, to flourish it's important to bet on yourself and practice good self-care. As you start to really bloom as a leader, however, your outlook will shift increasingly outward. You will practice and become expert at the true art of engaging with others. You will put relations and relationships at the center of your life. And you will go forth into the community and bring back a bountiful basket of perspectives that will enrich you, inspire you, and help you create something truly meaningful—for all.

For me, leading with meaning is an exercise in co-creation and service to another. As I always say, I serve to lead and I lead to serve. When I lead with meaning, I am genuinely leading in service to others. Which is why at its heart, leading with meaning always has a component of both service and engagement.

In 2005, I was part of the Target team that developed a campaign called "Dream in Color." The campaign was an invitation to our guests to imagine a world where diversity is widely celebrated and where people of all complexions and cultures express themselves freely. This initiative was Target's way of honoring voices past and present that inspire us to create a brighter future for all.

The campaign featured numerous celebrities and notable community leaders, including Emilio Estefan, Debbie Allen, Ming Tsai, Beth Takekawa, Louis Fonsi, Holly Robinson Peete, John Legend, and Dr. Maya Angelou. In addition to celebrating these icons, the "Dream in Color" initiative also offered free online lesson plans, resources, and curricula for teachers and community leaders. Dr. Angelou was featured in one of the earliest iterations of the campaign.

As a team, we had to determine who would interview Dr. Angelou. I was thinking that we would partner with a professional journalist like Oprah Winfrey or Barbara Walters. But as we brainstormed, my boss at the time, Michael Francis, suggested that I do it.

"You will be great, Laysha. I trust you," he said.

In my head I thought, "Well, I'm glad you trust me because I don't know if I trust myself."

But because of his confidence in me, I tried to settle myself down and prepare for the assignment. I told myself that even if I botched the interview, I would learn from the experience.

I conducted the interview at Dr. Angelou's home in Winston-Salem, North Carolina, in 2006. When I pulled into her driveway, I started thinking about the luminaries who had visited before me, and I didn't feel worthy. In fact, I was scared as hell, feeling like a total fake—and yet strangely excited. I knew the interview was going to end up in *Essence* magazine, a publication I'd admired and that had inspired me since I was a small child. I asked God to give me strength (and wanted to pray for a stiff drink but it was a little early for that and I was on the clock), and then took a deep breath and stepped out of the car and into the opportunity.

From the start, Dr. Angelou seemed comfortable sharing her space and wisdom with me and our team, which immediately put me at ease. The sista was spirited (take that as you will!). As we sat at her kitchen table, her honesty, eloquence, inimitable wit, warmth, and profound wisdom were on full display. She spoke openly of how her love of cooking helps foster relationships and creativity. I felt like I was hanging out with one of my aunties. Because we spent time just kicking it, by the time we got to the interview itself, which took place in her living room, the conversation flowed naturally. I was absorbing every word that Dr. Angelou said. There was something so safe and welcoming about being in her presence. I felt that rare feeling of my armor coming down.

I had a set of questions in front of me that had been revised, reviewed, and approved a thousand times over by a small army of professionals, and a list of things that needed to be accomplished, but I got lost in her responses on more than one occasion. She shared so many beautiful stories, I had to stay focused so I would have quality notes and quotes.

The most profound part of that day occurred, of course, through her words. We were talking about the importance of year-round service. She felt strongly that civic engagement was not something you reserved for a special occasion or holiday like MLK Day but something you did on a regular basis. She said, "As long as I am here, I will be of use."

As long as I am here, I will be of use.

As she continued to talk, I kept thinking about those words and coming back to them. And when I reviewed the interview later, the phrase stuck out for me once again. I knew it was striking a chord deep within. But I wasn't quite sure yet why or what she'd hit on that was resonating so deeply with me.

Over time, I came to realize why the sentiment meant so much to me: In just eleven brief words, Dr. Angelou shined light on my sense of purpose—illuminating and deepening it. In the process, she reaffirmed my commitment to how I want to live my life.

Those words have been with me ever since, a quiet mantra in my mind, moving me forward in the direction of my life's purpose to be in service to others. I've never wavered from the spirit of that message. As long as I am here, I will lead to serve. And I will serve to lead. I will be of use. I will be of use through my engagements with those who guide me and those whom I guide, who are sometimes the same people.

As we'll explore further below, the mantra to be of use does not distinguish between nonprofit work and for-profit work. I led to serve and served to lead at Target, and still do in my board member capacities, whether it's a for-profit board or a nonprofit one. For me, being in service to others is about an orientation to the community you are serving, not about the type of service you deliver. It is about understanding your chosen community and co-creating with them. It is about believing that the highest level of leadership is to *be of use* to those you are leading and serving. It's about engaging with others and finding meaning through that engagement.

At the end of the day, Dr. Angelou gifted me with an inscribed copy of her cookbook, *Hallelujah! The Welcome Table*. Throughout the book Maya's recipes are paired with amazing stories of her life through food, friends, family, and letters. You can feel her warmth on every page. And not only did she help me reinforce a standard for my sense of purpose, but she also inspired me to make her collard greens recipe every year on Thanksgiving or any other day when I just need food for my soul.

Expand Your Circle

The more you open up to the outside world, the more it opens up to you. And this means engaging with a wide range of people, as part of your job or simply as part of your life. Bernard Tyson, former CEO of Kaiser Permanente, taught me the value of reaching deep into the community to engage a wide variety of stakeholders. Please note that when I say wide, I mean different perspectives, different experiences, and a range of backgrounds; it's about quality, not quantity. When you meaningfully engage with your wider community, unexpected opportunities will often show themselves, potentially leading to better solutions.

Bernard's passion and purpose for health care began when he was a young man. He greatly admired the doctors who took care of his mother after a brief illness and was inspired by how they looked after his entire family. He initially wanted to become a doctor, but he later found his purpose in health care administration.

He and I worked closely together over the years through the Executive Leadership Council (ELC). He chaired the ELC board, and I chaired the ELC Foundation. At times, when I got pulled into the vortex of the Target bullseye, Bernard pushed me on the need to re-evaluate and reprioritize who I was spending my time engaging with. He had a diverse and eclectic set of relationships with people from all walks of life. Through his example, he enhanced my ability to keep my engagements diverse and wide. And while he valued everyone he spent time with, he clearly understood that some of those relationships were more unique and transformative than others.

Bernard often said to me, "Your Target relationships are important, but the bullseye will only take you so far." That was his way of telling me not to get too comfortable and to continuously invest in my relationships outside of Target. He wanted to ensure that I was taking a balanced approach—building relationships both inside and outside the organization. Bernard's point was for me to gain a broader perspective from a wider variety of people.

While considering another position or company was not the focus of building a collection of relationships, we would often swap stories about the interest we would receive from government, nonprofit, or other corporate organizations for employment. There was one time that I seriously considered one of these offers—because it came directly from Bernard, when he was CEO at Kaiser.

I greatly respected Bernard's leadership and focus on providing accessible, affordable, and equitable health care for everyone. Being aligned with that mission was something I felt like I could get behind and get up every day and be excited about. And being a direct report to a brotha? This would be rarefied space.

I said no in part because it was not the right time for my family. My husband Bill's father's health was declining, and my parents were aging, and I wanted to make sure that we could both be available. But also at that point, the advice Bernard had given me years before had paid off. My circle of contacts had continued to expand, and as a result of those relationships I had grown my ability to lead with meaning and I knew that there was more I could do at Target.

Bernard died unexpectedly a few months after our discussions about the role. He was just sixty years old. I was stunned and in shock.

Bernard's leadership and legacy live on because he practiced what he preached. I learned from him the importance of taking a long view of developing relationships and that leading with meaning is all about engaging far beyond our immediate circles. Bernard helped me understand that the world is wide and deep and the more I got out into it, the more opportunities I would see and could seize, always with the goal of serving others.

We will discuss increasing your connection currency in much greater detail in chapter 4, but for now I'd like you think about expanding your circle and your contacts.

- Who are your peers in the industry? Can you join an industry association, either local or national, and meet them? Are there Meetup or Facebook groups you can join?

- Is there a membership organization for your current field of interest, an adjacent one, or a field that you're interested in learning more about?

- Are there trainings and lectures outside the company you could attend?

- Are there conferences you could attend where you'd meet people with similar interests? When you go, show up ready to introduce yourself, meet people, and build a connection.

- Are there social clubs you could join, such as a sports team, a book club, or a wine club, where

> you'll meet people with whom you know you have
> one common interest, but which can expand to
> many others?
>
> Have fun with expanding your circle!

Engage Your Community's Insights and Co-create

Good community relations aren't just good people skills, they're a path to doing good business. Consistent engagement with local communities can spark ideas, increase exchange, and smooth the path for new developments. If you are getting out in the world and trying to understand your locality, you will automatically begin to find fresh opportunities to create solutions for the community and with the community. Leading with integrity and humanity requires additional insights and perspectives. Also, the more you learn from others, the more likely it is you will make decisions that have broader impact.

Understanding your local community is simply basic good business sense. Seasonal products are one example of this. The needs of folks in the climate of the Midwest might look very different than what is needed in the southern portion of the United States. The puffy winter coats you feature in January in a store in Minnesota might be replaced by a display of short-sleeved shirts in a store in Mississippi. Good businesses understand this and adjust their assortments accordingly. Great businesses go deeper and are continually fine-tuning their relevant products and services by engaging with and gaining insights into the wants and needs of their customers.

Insights

A few years after my meeting with Maya Angelou, I sat in yet another home filled with warmth and creativity. This time, I was in a bright, sunny Iowa kitchen. Delicious scents from the oven perfumed the air as the kitchen's owner, Judy, bustled around doing meal prep. Through the glass door, I could see a large outdoor garden overflowing with green fine herbs and tomatoes ripening on the vine. I even spotted some kale leaves poking up through the dirt, and flashed to my mother's garden back home in Indiana. Judy was explaining to me how she perfected her pie crust (the secret is a good pie shield, a protector that prevents the crust from burning or overbrowning) and how much she loved her new self-cleaning oven.

Now, I'm not a baker. And I wasn't contemplating changing professions. But I was taking notes during my visit with Judy; I was doing research. Talking to Judy, I was gaining invaluable insights into what a Target guest like her loved and how she lived her life. I asked questions about her preferences in an open-ended way, such as getting her to tell me about her morning routine. I was curious as to whether a guest like Judy preferred to drive to work or take public transportation, or whether she would get her coffee at Starbucks or a local coffee shop on her way to work. I would then record her answers. And I was often surprised by what our guests would say, such as the person who told me she prepared her coffee at home, despite all the coffee shops nearby, or the many people who told me they enjoy tea. Judy, like me, liked the ritual of stopping at a drive-up for coffee on her way to work. "Two creams, no sugar, could be my middle name," she joked.

Gathering insights and being curious about what our guests cared about and their daily habits and routines wasn't just about relationship-building, it also helped us offer relevant products and services. Spending a day with a guest like Judy, learning what ingredients she uses to make her meals, what laundry detergent she prefers, what she does and doesn't like about her appliances, and even what time of day it's easiest for her to go to the store, isn't just an exercise in customer relations, it's good business. As an insight expert (or someone who specializes in discovering insights about a company's guests) would say, the companies that succeed in today's environment are those that attract, retain, and deepen their relationships with their consumers or guests. For it is in those guests and their continued interest in the products that companies provide that the long-term value of a business lies.

When I first went to school for social work, I learned a great deal about participant observation, in-depth interviews, and focus groups. What I hadn't foreseen is just how handy all those tools would be when it came to my new career in business. I knew how important it was to understand our guests. As it turns out, the best companies are as interested in their guests as social workers and anthropologists are in the subjects of their studies. In business, as in the university or the social work profession, you can learn a great deal by studying others' behavior.

In today's highly competitive business environment, anyone can set up an online retail shop with just a few clicks. Buying can happen anywhere and goods can be delivered anywhere; as a result companies are always looking for even the slimmest competitive advantage.

Truly understanding your guest is a business imperative—and gives you an upper hand on the competition. Being in service to others has never been more important, no matter what business you're in.

You cannot be of use to your customers if you don't understand which messages or content or product/services are going to genuinely engage them. So you collect information on their attitudes (what they think or feel), on their demographics (who they are), and on their behaviors (what they do). You know whether Gen Z shops more at your store or at your competitor and for what goods. And you target people with similar characteristics to your best guests in the hope that they too will appreciate similar offerings and shop in ways that mirror your best guests.

This kind of information gathering on your guests isn't limited to retailers. Life Time is an athletic club with locations across the country. After one of their fitness classes, they will send a customer an email to learn more about their experience. They want to know if their guests had a good workout, if they felt the instructor was helpful and delivered a good experience, and if they feel Life Time is meeting their health goals. Some of this is to entrench consumers' loyalty and some is to collect useful feedback about what they're doing right and what they could be doing better. Life Time wants to be of use to their consumers.

Insight work isn't limited to for-profit companies. Many nonprofits and foundations use insight experts to gather data and help them act on data-driven insights. Insights help a nonprofit align what they do and their desired outcomes, for everything from providing low-income homebuyers with affordable housing to job training and workforce development.

In addition, many companies and nonprofits are no longer just tracking behaviors and attitudes. They're trying to anticipate them.

So, for example, if you bought bananas the last few times you shopped, a picture of bananas and an option to purchase them may automatically appear the next time you go to that store's website. And remember Judy's insights? We would use her consumer insights such as her preference for picking up her morning coffee on her way to work, along with additional primary and secondary research and data points, to anticipate new products and services we thought our guests would enjoy, such as ordering online or pickup in store or drive-up or home delivery. In fact, Target launched drive-up in 2017. By 2019, the service was available in all fifty states. And in 2020, Target added the ability to get fresh and frozen grocery drive-up, which turned out to be impeccable timing as the pandemic hit.

In both for-profits and nonprofits we often use good qualitative and quantitative research, to make sure that we are constantly on top of what our guests are looking for. And we cultivate a culture that embraces the importance of and use of the insights we've gathered. What our community thinks, wants, needs, and enjoys matters to us. We are leading to serve. And find meaning in that relationship-building and engagement.

Co-create

Beyond understanding your local community, you also benefit from engaging the local community on solutions to their unique challenges. This is co-creation. Co-creation involves not just acknowledging local needs but determining what those needs are and how to serve them. You are literally building something together. It's a fundamental tenet of how I lead with meaning. At Target, I co-created solutions with many stakeholders. And I serve on for-profit and nonprofit boards and volunteer for causes I care about—all of which require formal and informal engagement with a wide variety of people to co-create resolutions to issues. When we co-create we not only become better problem-solvers, but we also often open up opportunities we'd never before envisioned. True creativity can flourish as a result.

Even at the earliest stage of your career, you may be co-creating. Today, people coordinate and create over the internet. We problem-solve in Facebook and Reddit groups. We form alliances through LinkedIn, Instagram, and TikTok. Our community may or may not be in a specific locality. Others who share your purpose can be found internationally. Your community is how and where you define it. But the principle of co-creating remains the same: You open up opportunities by connecting and listening to your larger community.

As Target was preparing to expand into Harlem, New York, in the early 2000s, we understood the power of relationships and stakeholder engagement when entering a new market. We didn't want to move into these neighborhoods without getting to know the neighbors and learning the values of the community. I was charged with orchestrating Target's efforts to listen, learn, and co-create with the intention of being a positive addition to the community, not a diminishment. As I often say, we weren't just building a store in a community—we were building a store *with* a community. As a brand, we had learned over time to be humble enough to listen and wise enough to ask for help from the folks who knew best. I tapped into a group of well-established entrepreneurs and cultural experts who I ultimately referred to as my New York Crew.

The New York Crew included Bethann Hardison, a trailblazer and icon in the fashion industry (who also taught me how to throw back a few tequila shots—with class and style); Thelma Golden, director and chief curator for the Studio Museum in Harlem; Bevy Smith, television host, author, and entertainment reporter; Marcus Samuelsson, renowned chef, author, TV personality, and owner of the Red Rooster restaurant in Harlem and several others around the world; and Kim Hastreiter, journalist, editor, and cofounder of *Paper* magazine, who became my partner in hosting a series of dinners in the community. The New York Crew not only greatly assisted with Target's debut in the city, specifically in Harlem, but also became incredibly special in my life. We developed an open kinship where we could talk straight with each other. I was incredibly appreciative of the unfiltered, direct advice they gave me. And on top of that, each of them was simply great to hang with.

Each dinner was a gathering of twenty-five to thirty people hosted in honor of one of the iconic New York Crew leaders to celebrate their contributions to the unique treasure and asset that is Harlem. Kim and the guest of honor worked with us to curate the invite list, helping us ensure a diverse mix of guests with varied perspectives. By breaking bread together, we had the opportunity to hear from a variety of voices about what they believed was most special about Harlem and what aspects they wanted us to honor with our new store.

One early meeting was held at Marcus Samuelsson's new restaurant, Red Rooster, before he even opened the space. The walls were still unpainted white and the renovation with all its special Red Rooster touches was not yet in place. The goal was to honor the place, honor the space. And though it was still unfinished, we could already glimpse the vision Marcus had for a comfort-food gathering spot that would become a cornerstone of the community.

As usual, I was seeking to engage meaningfully with the community, and looking for insights into our guests. I knew that there was some initial resistance to a big-box store like Target joining the Harlem community. My goal was to get the real lowdown from the folks we'd gathered on how the community felt about having us come.

The smaller focus group of community leaders I'd assembled that day affirmed that there was indeed some resistance to our entry. Everyone, especially at that time, worried about gentrification. That wasn't a surprise. And we understood their fears.

But many people who lived in Harlem were excited about Target's arrival. They'd seen what we'd done elsewhere and knew we were a good neighbor. They were very aware that we would bring jobs. And that we would bring community investment beyond employment.

The community members who looked forward to our entry wanted a place to shop for affordable fresh food, for things that appealed to families, and for a fashion-forward assortment of reasonably priced clothing. Does that mean that people loved everything we did? No. Empathy and humility means admitting that you don't have all the answers. But the community leaders, like the residents, generally understood we could be part of the solution, not part of the problem.

Ultimately, we learned that we were an even better fit than we imagined. Harlem is a community of culture, and we were considered a more upscale discount store. People wanted a place to shop in their own neighborhood. They knew and loved the "Tarzhay" style. They were excited to have some of that Tarzhay magic in their community. We got a lot of credit for being aligned with Harlem's aesthetic.

The listening and learning naturally led us to start to co-create. Target's "flavor" naturally aligned with Harlem's. What if we could mutually inspire each other?

That first dinner laid the ground for future partnerships. I was already working with Thelma Golden, a trusted voice in Harlem. We were a company that considered artists part of the family, and I was truly excited to forge a partnership with her and the Studio Museum. Target sponsored Free Sundays at the Studio Museum in Harlem starting around 2008. But we knew we could do more. How could we make sure that we weren't displacing local businesses? How could we take our co-creation efforts further?

Our conversations led to special products and collabs with Isabel and Ruben Toledo, with Stephen Burrows, and of course, with Marcus Samuelsson. These collabs all resulted in unique products that reflected the design and culture of Harlem and the Harlem residents who brought their love of that community to their work and to the world. Isabel and Ruben Toledo's collection included psychedelic swimsuits and towels in cerulean blue that echoed the vibrant colors you'd find in the streets of Harlem. Stephen Burrows's knits embodied an urban street aesthetic and featured a zip-front pocketed hoodie dress. Marcus Samuelsson's collection included a range of practical kitchenware and tees that honored the community and were only available at the East Harlem Target store. We also started a Harlem designer collection that was available in East Coast stores. It wasn't easy, but despite the supply chain complications it was a wonderful way to celebrate the design heritage of the community.

We also followed the Dayton family tradition of doing well by doing good. Five percent of the purchase price of the special collab products went to a nonprofit of the designer's choice, which included El Museo del Barrio, and the Fund for Public Schools in support of libraries at the Young Women's Leadership School of East Harlem and P.S. 180 Hugo Newman.

I deeply enjoyed the conversations with my Harlem crew that led to these collabs. When you co-create you acknowledge that everyone has a perspective and you celebrate the expertise and the best that all parties can bring. Each gathering allowed us to learn what was already working well in the community, listen for what they needed, and thoughtfully co-create with Harlem residents about how Target could be a good neighbor and an integral part of the community and the culture of Harlem going forward.

These are negotiations. Practically you may need to give up things you thought you were attached to. But you often find even better solutions or acceptable compromises. You also gain a great deal when others feel that you have respected them and they feel heard.

When you're meaningfully engaging, as we did at our dinners, you're also creating a unique space in which true creativity can flourish. And trust is built. I had an opportunity to authentically share Target's story and my own. As we got to know each other, this allowed us to see each other's humanity—and to appreciate the importance of honoring culture.

Here are some tips for practicing co-creation:

- Enter into collaboration with a "we," not a "me," mindset.

- Make sure everybody who should be at the table is at the table (or in the Slack group, or the Discord group, or whatever virtual group you choose). Invite them in or make sure that their perspective is there via your research.

- Be actively engaged in executing the desired outcome. Help develop a project plan, participate in the fundraising, co-chair a committee, and/or be a spokesperson-advocate for the work.

- How could you mutually inspire and co-create with members of your organization or community?

- Have you gotten out into your community, virtually or in person, understood their wants and needs, and explored all your options for co-creating solutions and opportunities?

Co-creation is a stepping stone that can lead to authentic human connections, including powerful, transformative relationships like the ones I share even now with my New York Crew. This particular Harlem store has closed, but Target operates in Harlem to this day and the relationships live on. We turn next to how you can create an entire web of authentic connections and further increase your connection currency.

PS from Laysha

By its very nature, leading with meaning is a process of collaboration and engagement. We work with others to solve challenges. Along the way we build mutual empathy and understanding. As a result, opportunities we might never have envisioned develop, flourish, and bear fruit.

CHAPTER FOUR

Form Your Kitchen Cabinet

The ability to lead is directly affected
by the relationships a leader builds.

—CENTER FOR
CREATIVE LEADERSHIP

L ike many people, when I first went off to college, I wasn't quite sure what to expect. Who would I talk to? What would I possibly have in common with folks? How would I meet people? Then I met Reesie. Her real name was Theresa May Brown. Reesie was my college roommate and Alpha Kappa Alpha (AKA) Tau chapter sorority sister at Indiana University. She was from the relatively large (for me!) city of Indianapolis. Reesie had a wide smile and an infectious laugh. Her incredible sense of humor was matched only by her big heart.

She was also hugely resourceful. I have a picture of me, Reesie, and another roommate, Lisa Breen, all laughing together in our dorm room, sitting surrounded by our books, studying—at an ironing board! We needed a place to study for the times when the library was closed, and Reesie figured out that if we set up a table in our dorm room, we could still study. Of course, we didn't have a table that fit all three of us and our books, but Reesie told us to leave it to her. Like a magician doing a magic trick, she then pulled out the ironing board. Voilà! A study table that would fit all of us.

Reesie was going to be a teacher (and yes, of course, she succeeded). To know her was to be touched by her. She was always curious about people, asking questions about who they were and what made them tick. She thought everyone was worth getting to know and everyone was worth being nurtured. She was right. I learned from her that everyone, no matter how different they are from you, has something to offer, and everyone matters.

Reesie taught me that relationships are the core of a meaningful life and career. It's a lesson I've taken to heart for the entirety of my adult existence. No one creates a successful life or career alone. I've had the privilege of working with and being supported by an entire web of incredible mentors, allies, and advocates who have been essential to my personal and professional success. My relationships have buoyed me and transformed my life, almost beyond recognition.

Connection Currency

I know that many who see my job title or even know me will be surprised to hear that I'm not the social butterfly people assume I am. I'm more introverted than extroverted by nature, and it takes quite a bit of work for me to be "on." I had to learn to lean into my extroverted side to connect with a variety of different people across different sectors, and to master both the art and science of building the right collection of authentic relationships. It's been worth it.

Your connection currency—the social capital you accrue by developing authentic relationships—matters, because in life and leadership, it's your relationships that drive results and impact. So how do you build, grow, and sustain authentic life connections? I know that learning to build a portfolio of relationships and develop your connection currency may sound a bit daunting at first. But whether you're just starting out, or starting over in a new position at work or in life, it is entirely doable. We'll walk through the steps. Once you understand a bit more about the process, you too will be able to foster a genuine community of connected people who will celebrate your wins, comfort and counsel you in your defeats, challenge your assumptions, and champion you forward.

The Kitchen Cabinet

To develop your portfolio of connections, I always suggest thinking about who you want in your "kitchen cabinet." The U.S. President has a cabinet of advisors who counsel him, and maybe someday her, on a variety of subjects. With some thought, creativity, drive, and luck, you can build your equivalent. I use the term "kitchen" to refer to the fact that these are not formal positions you are signing people up for. Rather, you're seeking unofficial, private advisors. The term originates from the 1800s when a parallel government cabinet was set up after the purge of the more official cabinet.

The members of your kitchen cabinet are your most trusted advisors. They are the individuals you need right now to offer advice and inspiration. Your mentors will include experts, challengers, and reverse mentors. They will promote your learning, guide you to good decisions, and help you move your career forward. Your allies will include nurturers and members of your hype squad. Finally, there are your advocates, who will include sponsors and touchstones. These are the folks who can not only serve as a sounding board, support you, and stimulate your growth, but can walk you through doors you might otherwise not have been able to walk through.

How do you assemble this cabinet? The answer will look different at different career and life stages. The first presidential cabinet in the United States only had four members: the secretaries of state, war, and the treasury, as well as the attorney general. The current president has fifteen cabinet members, with an additional seven advisory positions of cabinet rank. You too can start small and expand as your needs grow.

I'll tell you how I assembled mine and offer some insights as we go. But also, please know that once you know what you're looking for, bringing together a cabinet might be easier than you'd suspect, even if you're a covert introvert.

Mentors

A mentor serves as both a counselor and coach. Mentors are trusted advisors from all walks of life who give you honest, direct, and candid feedback. They form the heart of your kitchen cabinet, especially in the earliest stages of your career. Mentors provide constructive feedback on challenges you face and point you toward opportunities that will help you learn and grow. They share their experiences and help amplify your superpowers, or your unique set of strengths and skills. They can be senior to you, peers, or junior to you in position, but skilled in ways that you may not be. Let's look at each type—*challengers*, *experts*, and *reverse mentors*—in turn.

CHALLENGERS

Michael Francis prepared me for a C-suite career well before I even knew what a C-suite was. If Bob Ulrich, the former Target CEO, was the kind of challenger who often exercised tough love, Michael embodied another style of challenging: He was a mentor who gently pushed me outside of my comfort zone and through doors that turned out to be more open than I ever expected.

Michael was Target's chief marketing officer during the company's ascension from regional low-cost player to iconic, design-focused national discount retailer in the early 2000s. Michael was not just a marketing genius, but a master communicator with unmatched skills in presentation and persuasion. He had a sixth sense when it came to trends and cool things Target ("Tarzhay") could do. He was never at a loss for words, and never missed a chance to make a connection, whether with a legendary rock star, a local entrepreneur, or the headquarters cleaning crew.

Michael was also the kind of leader who empowered his team. He was open to all kinds of ideas, no matter where they came from. He pushed us to think way outside the traditional retail marketing box and encouraged us to share ideas that scared us. He knew that if an idea made us nervous, it often meant it had real potential.

I had seen Michael's technique of challenging us play out in various meetings, but the way in which he pushed us to grow came into clear focus for me in the mid-2000s. At the time, strategic stakeholder engagement, particularly at the federal level, wasn't a top priority for Target. Stakeholder engagement is the process of cultivating relationships inside and outside of an organization (such as employees, elected officials, suppliers, community leaders, and nonprofit groups) with the goal of influencing their understanding of your organization and their actions related to your organization's goals. Because the company was growing rapidly, I suggested to Michael that we become more engaged on a national scale as befitted our growing brand presence. We were no longer just a Midwest company and I thought we should explore federal engagement in addition to the local outreach we were already doing. I had been doing some research on national organizations and associations and was especially curious about joining the presidential boards and commissions.

Presidential boards and commissions are the advisory groups of subject matter experts convened by the executive branch to provide advice and recommendations to the president, agency heads, and other staff. I knew that citizens had the opportunity to serve on the boards, albeit uncompensated. The appointment processes vary. I wasn't totally aware of it at the time, but I was entering a labyrinth. Some boards and commissions are presidentially appointed, while others are appointed by a specific agency. Some take direct applications, and in some cases the process of nomination is entirely murky. Reaching out to the stakeholders involved, however, is always crucial, as is finding expert guidance, the latter of which we'll get into with more detail below.

At the time, I was not in the C-suite, nor was I part of the leadership team at Target, but, true to his gently challenging approach, Michael encouraged me to do the research. He warned me up front he couldn't promise me Target would do everything I suggested, but he let me know that he would take my recommendations seriously.

Excited to make my initial suggestion of federal engagement a reality, I did my homework, working with an outside agency on multiple scenarios. We were looking at different organizations with a national presence relevant to our business and our leaders' skills and interests. I wanted to make sure that there was a good fit with whichever senior executive at Target ended up engaging with policymakers and influencers on the national stage; the best fit would allow us to represent our business as effectively as possible. I prepared a comprehensive matrix outlining recommendations of agencies we could be considered for, with priority given to the presidential boards and commissions.

I was excited about Target testing a new level in stakeholder engagement and looking forward to supporting the effort behind the scenes. So imagine my surprise when I presented my recommendations, and Michael said he supported moving forward with our application to the presidential boards and commissions, but not with any of the leaders on the matrix.

I was confused. We had thought through all the best possibilities about who should engage on the national stage, and I was sure we'd launch the opportunity with a member of our C-suite leadership team.

"Who did I miss?" I asked.

Michael said, "You."

I was stunned. Me? I had nowhere near the experience necessary. I was a fairly new company officer. I wasn't even on the leadership team. How could Target possibly send me to Washington, D.C.?

Michael countered by telling me I had an innate ability to create strategic connections. Michael and I went way back; we had initially worked together in Chicago. He had seen me in action and we both appreciated the power of connection. He said I had a way with "unusual suspects" in that I could engage effectively with both allies and detractors of the brand. Michael was both challenging me and encouraging me to build on this strength, knowing that it aligned with not just the company's purpose, but my own. I'd done the homework.

Challengers aren't always as encouraging as Michael was in this instance. Sometimes they're tougher on you and tell you all the hard truths. But you need those mentors in your life who will play devil's advocate, encourage you to think outside the box, challenge you, and sometimes push you out of the office and into the wider world so that you can have broader impact.

Figuring out who can play this role in your life may not be as difficult as it sounds. Who challenges you on a weekly, if not daily, basis? And do you see their challenges as opportunities or as threats? Perhaps you already have a challenger in your life, but it's you who needs a slight reframing, so that you're seeing the positive in their pushes. Yes, it can feel uncomfortable to associate with those you are not used to associating with, or to be held accountable in ways you never have before. But having folks around you who consistently challenge you to go to unfamiliar places and spaces is a necessary part of continuous growth.

EXPERTS

Experts have the specialized knowledge you need to fill in the gaps in your education. These mentors are often specific to a certain stage of your life or career. Sometimes they are just there for you in the moment; sometimes they become lifelong friends.

Kassie Davis was my boss when I was working at Marshall Field's in Chicago as a community relations manager. Kassie had an MBA and was very business-savvy, with a keen understanding of strategy and a deep financial acumen. As mentioned earlier, at the time I was new to the business world and interested in becoming a bridge between the company and the community. Kassie knew that having a basic understanding of financial terms was important for me to be successful. She taught me the fundamentals: what a profit and loss statement was, how to read a balance sheet, how to calculate our cash flow, market share, and ROIC (return on invested capital). She also helped me understand retail-specific concepts like comparable store sales (the revenue generated by a retail location in the most recent accounting period relative to the revenue it generated in a similar period in the past), the cost of goods sold, the gross margin (the portion of a company's revenue left over after direct costs are subtracted), and the inventory cost/markup.

Kassie also encouraged me to learn more outside the company. As a result, I took a few strategic planning and nonprofit financial management classes at the Donors Forum of Chicago, which connected more dots for me. It also connected me to an incredible network. Ultimately, as Kassie had predicted, this early financial tutelage, from Kassie's informal teaching to the formal courses, prepared me for my role as a bridge to the community, and even for my later years in the C-suite and on nonprofit and corporate boards.

Kassie shared her expertise with me because she was a smart, capable leader who wanted the people working under her to be effective in their roles. I had proven myself as someone worth mentoring. I had crushed my sales goals in my previous position. I had demonstrated drive and curiosity. I was an eager, avid student, and I soaked up all the knowledge she was offering, which mattered. The more you show others your willingness to learn, the more willing they'll be to invest in teaching and mentoring you.

People also like to see that you've committed. You aren't necessarily signing up for a lifelong marriage to the industry you're in, but if you're at least sending signals that this is where your energy is going for the foreseeable future, it helps. Consciously or unconsciously, many in the mentor role are looking to help people succeed at doing the work they've already done. Your commitment to the values, expertise, and life they've chosen helps bolster their commitment to you. Also, it's worth remembering that they get social capital out of the relationship too. If you come across as someone who's going to be around in a few years, that can be a valuable connection for them. Make no mistake: Many mentors mentor solely out of the goodness of their heart. But it's worth noting that you may have a stronger shot at getting someone to mentor you and share their expertise if you are as genuinely committed to using that expertise and furthering the goals of the company, career, or industry as they are.

Another expert mentor was Ron Kaufman. Ron is a funny, irreverent guy. He's an insider's insider. The ideal D.C. connection, Ron always knows the scoop. He also knows all the rules, including which ones can be broken and which ones absolutely can't. He was exactly the kind of expert—and person—I needed to know as I waded into the unknown waters of working with the federal government.

Ron was the regional and then national political director of the Republican National Committee (RNC) under President Ronald Reagan. He went on to serve in President George H. W. Bush's administration as deputy assistant to the president for political affairs. We'd met when I was doing my initial research on presidential boards and commissions and was working with a public policy management firm called Dutko Worldwide. Dutko employed people like Ron who had been in both Republican and Democratic administrations and knew how the heck the complex process of appointment to presidential boards and commissions worked. I needed someone to explain the process to me: What attributes were the people who made the appointments looking for? What were the risks and challenges to a company like ours in applying to be part of a presidential board or commission? Was it another full-time job? I needed both an expert and a challenger, and Ron Kaufman perfectly fit the bill.

Like Michael, Ron felt I should be the Target representative. As part of our work together, we'd had many meetings and conversations with business leaders, elected officials, and community influencers, and he knew I was capable of engaging with and influencing leaders from a variety of backgrounds and experiences. He personally promised to guide me through an appointment to the agency Target and I were being considered for, AmeriCorps, then called the Corporation for National and Community Service (CNCS).

Ron more than kept his word. There were extensive interviews with the administration, much more extensive than I realized, and many steps to the process, some that made me downright uncomfortable. For example, my appointment required that I identify my personal party identification. Now, these appointments are supposed to be national community service and thus to be made regardless of one's party identification. In my view, my party ID had nothing to do with my role and I shouldn't have to divulge this information. Not to mention, George W. Bush was in the White House at the time, and I was worried I was going to be scrutinized on this basis alone. I began to worry that, surely, I was the wrong representative for Target to send after all. I was ready to put up a fight over this invasion of my privacy.

Ron heard me. He sat me down and coached me through the series of interviews I was about to undergo as part of the approval process, and he addressed this particular step, which had me all up in my feelings.

"Don't overthink it," he advised. "It's a customary part of the process. Besides, you don't need to worry. You're an 'approved D.'"

An "approved D"? I'd never heard that term before. I burst into laughter. Ron further explained that they were asking for my party ID precisely because they were trying to make the CNCS equally representative. His counsel helped me see it was important to answer the question. And that there would be no repercussions to identifying my party affiliation.

He also explained that the FBI would be investigating me for a background check and walked me through what that process would be like. He explained that they would interview a select number of people in my life to make sure I was worthy of a presidential appointment. It was another step of the process that might seem ordinary to those more familiar with public service, but it sent a stake of worry through my heart.

At the time, I did not know where my brother was. Back then, he had disappeared from our lives. And though now he is an active and much-loved member of our family, at the time, I was worried. What was I going to tell the FBI? I wasn't going to make something up. And what if they searched for him? I had no idea what they would find. Again, Ron stepped into the breach and offered solid advice.

"Just tell them the truth," he said. "Who knows, they might even discover his whereabouts."

I did as Ron advised. And the FBI did find my brother! Once again, Ron had steered me well: My honesty meant that at least on the government front, there would be no repercussions. I was appointed to CNCS/AmeriCorps under the George W. Bush administration and went on to serve during the Obama administration.

You never know who can come into your life as an expert, or as a challenger. Ron was both—and an unlikely ally. Mentors come in many forms, and it's a lesson in the importance of being receptive to others, even those who come to the table with very different perspectives. You never know who might turn out to be an invaluable shepherd; you need to stay open to all possibilities. I owe Ron the greatest debt. Without his expert guidance, I would never have served all those years. And I'm incredibly proud and grateful to have done so.

REVERSE MENTORS

Mentors aren't always our elders. Sometimes it's those who are younger than we are who can bring us the freshest insights. Once you've climbed your way up the ladder, your employees will often tell what you want to hear rather than what you need to hear. Young people, however, can sometimes tell us important truths—and, as we stay in the workforce longer and longer, can help bring us up to date.

Alana Hinkston was one such reverse mentor for me. Alana was a marketing associate at Target who has since gone off to get her MBA at Harvard. When we first met, I was just getting on social media. I was on a Minnesota Orchestra committee for a program to celebrate Nelson Mandela's centenary. Alana knew I was going off to South Africa and her advice was both diplomatic and straightforward.

"You know what, Laysha, your social media just isn't very good," she told me pointedly one day. "The type of pictures you take, the lighting, the quality. I know you say you don't particularly enjoy social media, but I think if you upped your game, you'd not only communicate with the public better, you might also start to have more fun with it."

Ouch. She'd nailed it. I wasn't a huge social media fan. I hadn't been either an early or a particularly eager adopter. But Alana and I had built up enough of a relationship that I appreciated her honesty. I knew she had good intentions, and I was grateful for her straight-no-chaser approach. Not everyone is comfortable taking on this role of reverse mentor, but if you have a good relationship with your team leader, I highly recommend speaking up as Alana did.

We went online and looked at lots of examples so that I had better sense of what she was talking about. Then she gave me homework: When I went to South Africa, I was to practice taking better pictures, try doing some video, use hashtags, and push myself to think about how to better capture the stories I wanted to share. With Alana's guidance, my social media became much more intentional and—she was right—much more enjoyable and successful.

A tip to those of you young enough to fill the reverse mentor role: If you want to be effective, remember that the goal isn't to criticize your elders. Be respectful. What Alana did particularly well was that she offered up context. She told me exactly how I could improve. It was constructive critique in service of helping me get better. She didn't sugarcoat my lack of social media skills, but showed me what others were doing well and offered specifics on how I could polish my presentation. She still occasionally DMs me on Instagram with praise, saying, "You've come such a long way," and with the occasional tidbit of advice on how I can publish even more distinctive posts. I may still need work, but her reverse mentoring dramatically improved my social media.

Allies

Not all the members of your kitchen cabinet are there to strategize. Often you need individuals who are providing more of a support function. Note that I am using the word "ally" slightly differently here from the current understanding of allyship, in which individuals with privilege use that privilege to support those from more marginalized communities. I use allies here to refer to the folks who lift you up, and on whom you can lean. Assemble as many of them as you can.

Allies can often be found in unexpected places. That person you thought you had nothing in common with. The person who started the same day and sat next to you at orientation. The other person in the office who is just as ambitious as you are.

When you first start out at a job, you may feel competitive with your peers. But your peers from even the earliest stages of your career will often turn out to be longtime allies who understand you, the colleagues—and bosses—you share, and the challenges you mutually face. Not to mention those peers in the trenches with you. They, more than anyone else in your life, often understand the nitty-gritty of your business—and are struggling to grasp the same changes and fresh opportunities in the industry that you are. My advice is to turn those feelings of competitiveness into allyship whenever and wherever you can. Which isn't to say you shouldn't listen to your instincts: Not everyone has caught on to the wisdom of taking the high road, and some people will misuse your confidences to advance themselves. If after several encounters your gut is still saying it won't be a mutually beneficial relationship, it probably won't be. But most of your peers are as eager for support as you are, and if you can bolster each other, and regularly exchange tips and information, everyone will benefit. I know I benefited from exchanges with my peers. You will help each other advance and grow. You may even become lifelong allies.

Allies take the form of *individual nurturers* or *hype squads*.

INDIVIDUAL NURTURERS

Individual nurturers are allies who might be there for a long stretch of your life and career—or even for its entirety. This might be a loyal assistant, a trusted peer, or even a family member, like my sister, Laynita, who has always supported me in my ambitions. We all need those individuals who will say: I believe in you, I support you, and I have your back. Individual nurturers are there for you and see the best in you.

A trusted longtime peer, Eric Erickson, and I were nurturing allies for each other. Eric, a creative director and visionary, has been a part of my journey for decades. We first met in the mid- to late 1990s when we were both leaders in marketing, reporting to Michael Francis. Eric was a true partner in my success, helping me advance and grow by supporting my ideas and bringing my programs and projects to life through clever and impactful marketing campaigns. He was someone I could bounce ideas off and he always freely shared his ideas to make my work better.

Eric understood that while at work, due to the nature of my public-facing roles, I was more extroverted, but that I am also very introverted, as is he. With Eric, I could be more outward—or more inward. On one occasion, when I hit a wall and couldn't be "on" anymore, Eric and his wife, Peggy, invited Bill and me to a family home they had in Red Lodge, Montana. Eric knew I would benefit from being in a place where I didn't have to go to endless meetings or give a speech at an event or make conversation at a large dinner. His Red Lodge dwelling was a place where I could curl up on a window seat with a good book and enjoy my leisure—and my freedom. It was a relaxing refuge, where I could recharge my batteries by turning off. And as my friend and ally, Eric knew that that was exactly what I needed.

Our support was mutual. When Eric's son, Kyle, passed away of cancer in 1998, we had a deep discussion about his life and career and the impact he wanted to make. Eric found purpose in the work the Children's Cancer Research Fund was doing, and I helped him join the board. Over the years, we partnered on many exciting projects, for which Eric designed memorable marketing campaigns, from Target House at St. Jude Children's Research Hospital to Target's billion-dollar education commitment. And in 2023, as I was preparing to retire from Target, I asked Eric to be a partner in the creation of my personal brand beyond the company. With the great care and strategic intent that he applied in his work as VP of creative at Target, Eric asked questions, listened, and helped me prepare for the next chapter. He has always had my back and I have always tried to have his.

HYPE SQUADS

Sometimes your allies are a group of friends you've assembled who act as your hype squad. These are your supporters and cheerleaders. Both men and women need other people in their lives who believe they are a big deal. And if there's one thing better than a single nurturer, it's a whole squad of them.

If you can assemble such a tribe, people you share common values or culture or interests with, and create community with them, your life will immediately change for the better. Perhaps you've found camaraderie with the players on your pickup basketball team or on the pickleball court, maybe you've discovered community with a group of fellow parents you met at the playground, or perhaps you're still in touch with college friends with whom you have a special bond. For me, there has always been something incredibly special about connecting with other women, especially Black women.

From my days of pledging AKA with my line sisters, the Twenty P.E.A.R.L.S., to my membership in The Links Inc., to bonding with the Sistas Connecting group at Target, there is something to be said about connecting with another Black woman who shares my lived experience and can relate to the unique challenges of the intersectionality of race and gender. When I see another Black woman whom I can genuinely connect with, I just know that that sister will help me keep moving forward and put one foot in front of the other in service of my purpose.

In 2020, as the pandemic was becoming all too real and many of us were looking for opportunities to connect virtually, I touched base with my friend Shaundra about bringing a group of Black women together for support and fellowship. Our goal was to create a virtual safe space to collectively process what was happening all around us.

We wanted to provide opportunities for intimate, personal, vulnerable conversations, so we decided to keep the group small. The idea was to create a space for connection that would allow each of us to show up as both executives and human beings, with the freedom and safety to share and say whatever was on our minds through the easy and natural shorthand of our common sisterhood. We would not have to translate for each other because we would just "get it" by virtue of each of us being Black and female in corporate roles.

Within a few weeks of reaching out and connecting with potential group members, we formed a group of ten Black female executives from all over the country: Shaundra, Susan, Wanji, Arlene, Nancy, Leilani, Julia, Kim B., Kim S., and me. We had different educational experiences and family situations, but we had all taken on major roles as business and community leaders. Though most of us are close in age and career stage, our group includes both mothers and aunties, and married and single women. We believed our group should have a badass name, and thus the Mocha Moguls collective was born.

During our first Zoom conversation, we agreed that there would be no agendas and no note-taking. These were off-the-record conversations unless we agreed otherwise. We offered a "come as you are, come when you can, and get what you need" invitation. No one had to justify missing a session or arriving late. With all the pressures we were facing, none of us needed that.

Each session opened up with a check-in on how everyone was doing or what was new. From there, our hours-long conversations would range from the serious to the sublime—and sometimes included an adult beverage. We talked about how we were adjusting to working virtually and we grappled with the disproportionate impact of COVID in the Black community. We also discussed the new and evolving ways of working, leading, and living during a pandemic that our companies and employees were grappling with.

When the COVID vaccines became available, we shared ideas for ways to convince vulnerable or elderly family members to get vaccinated. I had some of my first conversations about virtual funerals as several Mochas had to cope with losses within their families and their larger communities. It was very sobering to hear what it was like for my friends to attend these services for the first time—and later I had to do the same.

On the flip side, we had the joy of hearing from Mochas who were newly dating online in a pandemic world. During one session, one of the Gen Z daughters of a Mocha did an entire seminar on Bitcoin for us, and in another, a Mini Mocha (a very young daughter of a Mocha) practiced her music recitals. With little to no preplanning, we had interesting and dynamic discussions, every time.

Our conversations established the Mochas as a safe place for each of us to be vulnerable when we needed to be and supportive when others needed it. And it was a good thing, too, because the deaths of Ahmaud Arbery, Breonna Taylor, and George Floyd, among too many others, heightened the need for a sacred space, just for us, to process and share our feelings—a place to explore what it meant for us to lead our companies and support our communities at a time of monumental grief, anger, and seismic change. As Black business leaders, we were determined to transform a moment into a lasting movement—no matter how exhausted we were.

Black folks often say, "I see you," and I believe that we greet each other this way because we often aren't seen, heard, respected, or valued in ways that are real and meaningful outside of our immediate communities. I don't think I knew initially how much I needed to be seen, heard, respected, and valued by the Mochas without judgment or the need for translation.

By the time our weekend Mocha Mogul calls came around, I was eager for the genuine conversation, following long days of giving my best at work, feeling like I needed to be "on" and strong despite what was happening in the world. But with the Mochas it was OK to just be. To fill my cup and pour into theirs.

It's not that I wasn't supported by people whom I loved deeply, like my husband, my sister, or colleagues doing the genuine work. But because many of the Mochas are also the most senior Black person in their organizations, we could easily relate to one another on a different level. When we said, "I see you, sis," we meant it. The sisterhood of the Mochas was therapy for my mind and body, and a balm for my soul.

I've always believed that I have to force myself to move through difficult moments faster than I might like because of the positions that I occupy professionally, personally, and within the community. We can't all have a meltdown at the same time, right? There simply aren't enough spaces yet for Black women to be all up in our feelings, so we just don't let ourselves go there.

But the Mochas reminded me that, as Black women, we can create our own spaces to be, to feel, and to commune with others who share our values and lived experiences.

Creating a safe space, as we did with the Mocha Moguls, is about suspending judgment and being open, welcoming, and accepting . . . it's about finding a space where you can take the armor off. In one session we would talk through the joys and challenges of online dating, and in the next we shared tears and grief related to online funerals and the ongoing racial reckoning throughout the country. It's critical to build your support network to be a safe haven for advice, laughter, tears, joy, pain, celebrations, and everything in between.

Advocates

Your advocates are the Aunties and O.G.s, who, as their nicknames suggest, are the more experienced folks, the Original Gangstas or Old Guard, at least compared to you, who show up in your life at an opportune moment and then often remain for a more sustained period. They include your *sponsors*, who play an active role in advancing your career, and what I call your *touchstones*, who may leverage their connections and influence to benefit you, though that's not necessarily their primary purpose. By sparking your purpose within, touchstones are often responsible for the most important transformations in your life.

SPONSORS

Sponsors are your advocates. They might be your boss, though not every boss is your sponsor. Sponsors are in the mix and advocating for you at various stages of your career. Like mentors, sponsors are people you've made enough of an extended positive impression on that they are willing to extend a hand back. Unlike mentors, however, sponsors are directly positioned to help you advance and elevate your career. As discussed in the introduction, I believe that sponsorship is a crucial part of good management and leading with meaning. Good leaders are always looking to actively promote and lift up those whose talents have been confirmed through their work. Championing the impact of others is a key part of meaningful management and leadership.

Sponsors don't come out of nowhere. They are often people who have been mentoring or coaching you all along. They believe in you and your talents. They are your cheerleaders as well as your challengers. Michael Francis was a mentor and challenger who ultimately became a sponsor for me. Sponsors are often people who take special interest in you early on. Your response to their initial interest may then affect your future far beyond what you can initially see. Your connection currency accumulates interest like any sound investment. When it pays off is not always predictable or in your control. But if you keep investing in the relationship, it will pay off.

You may or may not be aware of it when a sponsor advocates for you. Michael Francis worked behind the scenes at multiple stages to let others know that I was capable and ready for the next stage of my career. He ultimately became a major advocate and sponsor for my ascension to the C-suite. I don't think my advancement would have happened without him.

Which isn't to say I could see all that at the time. Sponsors aren't always able to be that transparent. In some cases, you may not even know they are sponsoring you. You can discuss your goals and desires with your sponsor, but ultimately there may be limits to how much you can discuss whether they are or aren't advocating for a particular position for you. Much more important is to just continue doing the work and seeking out the growth that will position you as a strong leader, whatever your goals are.

TOUCHSTONES

Your touchstones are true Aunties and O.G.s. Like sponsors, they have seniority, power, and influence in the world. But touchstones are distinct lights. They are in the room where things happen, and those rooms might be inside or outside your company, but unlike sponsors they are rarely directly advocating for your ascension in a company or workplace. Like Mrs. King, they may not even have direct influence over your career or your advancement. Rather, by seeing you, understanding you, and sparking your purpose within, they are often responsible for the most important transformations in your life.

Once you find a touchstone, it's important to nurture them. They are often a bit intimidating when you first meet (remember, you must get comfortable being uncomfortable and take relationship risks!), but you may be surprised at how easy it can be to build a connection with them. Bruce Dayton, part of the founding family of the Dayton-Hudson Corporation, now Target, was one of my touchstones extraordinaire. When I had my first lunch with him, he asked me where I grew up. I told him Fountain City, the tiny town in Indiana where I was raised. I thought he would quickly move on to the next topic, but surprisingly, he was genuinely interested and wanted me to tell him more about my life there. It turned out that Bruce was born and raised in Minneapolis in the early 1900s, when it was a much smaller town, too. I hadn't expected to have anything in common with the man, and yet we'd already found a point of contact in our origin stories.

My touchstones like Mrs. Coretta Scott King, Mr. Bruce Dayton, and legal genius and civil rights icon Vernon Jordan have handed me hard truths when I needed to hear them. They have steered me through my education, pushed me forward into my first career opportunities, talked me through life transitions, and taught me powerful lessons.

They weren't just mentors, sponsors, and allies, though they guided me on my career path. Rather, touchstones occupy a unique place—one that business connections and friends can't necessarily fill—because their primary role in your life is to ignite your sense of purpose. Your touchstones ensure that you step up to your full capabilities and that you never stop leading with meaning.

Stakeholder Mapping

By now, you might have some ideas on who you could approach to include in your kitchen cabinet. Or maybe you need to do a bit more brainstorming. Either way, I suggest engaging in a more formal stakeholder mapping process. It will help you generate even more ideas for who you need and who you want to ask to participate in your cabinet. All you need is a pen and a piece of paper.

Stakeholder mapping was a routine part of my job at Target. As Target's chief external engagement officer, I was responsible for developing and nurturing relationships that advanced business objectives, enhanced reputation, and mitigated risks, as well as creating a streamlined, enterprise-wide approach and process for identifying, assessing, and engaging stakeholders that was applied across the business. You could say my entire job was building connection currency.

The process I describe below for forming your kitchen cabinet and building your connection currency is adapted from the stakeholder engagement process I've used professionally. This approach has helped me navigate all the relationships in my life. I strongly believe that by following the steps, at any stage of your career, you will open doors to new relationships, including the ones that can change your life.

The Five Steps

In forming your kitchen cabinet, you may be seeking mentors, allies, or advocates. Use these five steps to identify and engage these informal advisors.

STEP 1: SET GOALS

Like any important work where you want to have an impact, you have to set goals before you begin your relationship-building. The more specific you are in your goals, the easier it will be to identify the exact right connection to help you achieve those goals. For example, you might be looking for an expert mentor to help you develop a specific skill or a sponsor at work to help you elevate your visibility and take on more responsibility. Or maybe you've decided you want to be more strategic about sustaining authentic human connection by forming a hype squad or becoming a nurturer. Whatever your situation, take the time to identify and write down your goals.

STEP 2: IDENTIFY

Once you know your goals, make a list of your connections and identify relevant mentors (subject matter experts, challengers, reverse mentors), allies (nurturers, hype squad), and Aunties/O.G.s (touchstones and sponsors) among the people you view as close colleagues, friends, community connections, and family. You don't have to capture everyone you know, but cast a wide enough net so you can see the depth and breadth of your valued connections. Then you will begin to understand who you have—and who you need.

STEP 3: FILL IN YOUR GAPS

Identify your gaps based on the goal(s) you're trying to accomplish. Look beyond those who will merely reflect you back to you. As Mrs. Coretta Scott King often said to me, "Don't just surround yourself with people who look like you, act like you, think like you, or talk like you." That's not making true human connections . . . that's living in an echo chamber, and there's too much of that in our world already. If you feel stuck, try asking yourself some discovery questions to determine who belongs where in your map:

- Does this person have wisdom, knowledge, insights, or experience that I can learn from, even if, *and especially if,* it's divergent from mine?

- Will this person be direct and honest with me regardless of our roles, lived experience, and life stage? Will they challenge and strengthen my thinking?

- Are they subject matter experts in critical areas I need to learn more about, and if so, what skills do I hope to learn from them?

- Do they have the influence and connections to serve as a sponsor for me, or are they better equipped to be a mentor and work with me behind the scenes?

- How will *they* benefit from the relationship? Reciprocity is a key characteristic of successful relationships.

- What is my desired outcome? This is a really important one. You have to know what you want from a relationship, even if the outcome is simply to absorb knowledge and experience from someone you admire. Be clear and specific so you can monitor progress.

STEP 4: PRIORITIZE

Prioritize your list by identifying who you'd like in your closest circle of advisors. Reminder: It's quality over quantity. This isn't about building the biggest cabinet of advisors—it's about building the right cabinet for your needs at this time in your journey.

STEP 5: ACTIVATE

With a clear goal, a categorized list of connections, a plan to fill in the gaps, and a custom-designed kitchen cabinet, the next step is to engage with your connections. Determine when and how often to connect—and activate your plan to find and initiate new connections. Some tips based on my experience:

- Approach every relationship authentically and strategically. Authentic relationships can be strategic and vice versa. These are not mutually exclusive concepts. You can be sincere and approachable—and have strategic intent, whether you're engaging with a lifelong touchstone or meeting someone new for the first time.

- Lead with respect and humanity. By demonstrating respect and civility in every interaction, we lay a firm foundation for authentic human connection. Enter conversations with no judgment. See the person as they are—not who you want or expect them to be. Be open to hearing their perspective and set the table for a courageous conversation. By seeking to understand other people's stories and lived experiences, we're able to connect with them in a truly authentic way.

• Be a student and a teacher. You have something to learn and receive, and something to teach and give. Be open to teaching, sharing, and learning something new in every interaction.

• Some relationships will be sustained, some transactional—and that's OK. Transactional relationships—in work and in life—can be of great benefit. I often make a connection with someone because of knowledge and skills they have that I want to learn. I am forthcoming about what I want to learn from them—and offer to reciprocate if there is anything I can provide for them. When we accept that there is a season and a reason for every relationship, we can avoid agonizing over natural endings.

• Learn how to deliver a strategic yes. And a strategic no. Building connection currency takes time and effort, so don't waste yours. Think critically about where and how you want to engage and don't overcommit yourself. A strategic no might be "Not now, how about later," or "No, but here's a different way I can help you." This is especially important as work relationships become friendships and vice versa. It can be uncomfortable to tell someone no, but when it's delivered in the right way, everyone wins.

• The ultimate decision is yours. Your chosen connections are important advisors for your life and leadership learning journey—but they have a voice, not a vote. The ultimate decisions about your journey are yours to make. You are the CEO of your life and you get to make the calls.

Building your kitchen cabinet—and your connection currency—is not one and done, but rather an ongoing, lifelong process. These are not lifetime appointments unless you (and they) choose for them to be. Keep monitoring and adjusting who is in your kitchen cabinet, just as the president does! This is a dynamic body of support that will change as you change, growing or shrinking in response to what you need at any given stage of your personal growth or professional development.

Now that you've started the ongoing process of building your connection currency, let's turn next to some additional tools that will help you work well and live well.

PS from Laysha

Real leadership and growth emerge from our willingness to ask for help and give it. Authentic human networks are built on a balance of vulnerability and strength, trust, and acceptance of the idea that we'll all get better together.

PART THREE

WORK WELL, LIVE WELL

CHAPTER FIVE

Move Forward To Growth

One can choose to go back toward safety
or forward toward growth. Growth
must be chosen again and again; fear
must be overcome again and again.

—ABRAHAM MASLOW

I n this part, we will examine some of the tools you'll need to lead with meaning. These are business and life fundamentals you should know and use, whatever your chosen field or stage of your life and career. These techniques and skills are part of every sound leadership practice. When you lead with meaning, you will still be expected to further the growth of your organization as well as your own growth. Having effective tools will help you actualize your purpose.

Get Comfortable Being Uncomfortable

As you define and redefine your purpose, you will find yourself pursuing new opportunities, which is often an uncomfortable experience.

You will meet new people and try to understand where they are coming from, and that requires effort. You will take risks, not all of which will succeed. This is all perfectly normal. As we grow and change, we are forced out of our comfort zone. I always advise people to get comfortable with being uncomfortable. Discomfort often means you're on the right track. Risk is never far from opportunity.

Mike Hyter showed me this truth. Mike was the first Black man I met in executive leadership at the Dayton-Hudson Corporation. I was in my twenties, in a junior role at the company, and still living in Chicago. Mike was the vice president of community and government affairs at our Minneapolis headquarters. I had recently advanced from being a department manager to a community relations manager when Mike first reached out to get to know me. Eventually, he even invited me to visit our base in Minneapolis.

When Mike first reached out in the early 1990s I wasn't thinking about, or even recognizing, the opportunities his interest and support offered. At the time, I believed that the Windy City was the center of the universe—I'd never even been to Minneapolis. Pursuing a career in business still wasn't something I was completely sure about; it probably also scared me a bit. As I've previously described, back then corporate America didn't feel like a space that was designed for me. While I was enjoying the work and open to learning and doing more, I didn't know how I fit in it. I didn't look like anyone (other than Mike) at the corporate level, and I was still considering a career that I thought might be a better fit with my purpose of being of service.

Mike took me under his wing and showed me what was possible. From the start, he engaged me in higher-level strategic thinking, talking to me about things like annual plans and long-term plans, quarterly earnings, and the importance of developing high-performing teams, demonstrating that even though there weren't a lot of people who looked like us, there was still a *place* for us. I wasn't sure that I believed in that, but I did believe in him.

One of the ways he did this was by inviting me to meetings where I was junior to most of the other people in the room, and encouraging me to participate and provide my input, alongside my immediate supervisor. At the time, I remember thinking as I looked around the room at all the white men and women at levels well above mine, "What the hell am I doing here?" I wondered if my boss would be annoyed that I was included—in the room and in the conversation. I worried that I would say the wrong thing and look like a fool.

Now, it's true that you need to be mindful of context: If you're in a strictly hierarchical workplace, it is important to observe at first and get a sense of when speaking up is welcome, and when it isn't. It's always valuable to "read the room," especially when you are new. But assuming you are being mindful of context, don't be afraid to use your voice. In my experience, many people, especially when they are first starting out, aren't too talkative; they're too quiet. They self-censor much more than necessary. When I was hesitant to speak up, Mike reminded me that my voice was important in the conversation and thanked me for my contributions. Eventually, being in those spaces—listening, learning, and practicing leadership—I began to feel more comfortable and confident. By gently testing the boundaries of speech in the meetings you attend, you may learn that your input too is welcomed. And you will gain the confidence you need to continue participating and leading, even if the room doesn't have someone as generous and encouraging as Mike in it.

You will also occasionally learn where the boundaries are. And that's OK too. One of the most memorable moments in my relationship with Mike happened when he invited me to lunch at the Oak Grill in Minneapolis. It was one of my first fancy business lunches.

The Oak Grill was a dark and cozy dining room with fireplaces and fancy woodwork. It was known for its piping hot, buttery popovers that came with every meal.

The conversation flowed naturally. As we continued to talk and eat, I noticed that Mike had a particularly good-looking piece of meat on his plate. I'd gotten into the habit when I went out to restaurants with college friends of routinely sharing entrees and eating off each other's plates. Without waiting for Mike's permission, I stabbed the chunk of meat with my fork and took a bite. My memory of how good it tasted is diminished by my recollection of what happened next.

Mike froze, a look of shock on his face, and my insides twisted. I immediately knew I'd violated some kind of code. Someone else might have ignored it and silently formed a judgment or written me off for good. But instead, Mike gently said to me, "This will likely not be the last time you eat off my plate, but next time you just ask."

I was grateful that he didn't shame me and that he took the time to make it a teachable moment. Even though I had made a mistake, I felt seen, heard, and respected in a way I had never felt at work before.

Mike saw my potential beyond my rough edges. He gave me the freedom to be perfectly imperfect, knowing that my mistakes weren't what defined me. He saw me excelling and knew that there was potential under my naivete and lack of sophistication. Fast-forward twenty-five years, Mike and I have shared that story publicly many times to show young professionals that you can survive lapses in judgment with the right support. You can learn not to repeat mistakes. You can experience uncomfortable moments; you will learn and grow.

Over the years, Mike has continued to invest in me from afar and encouraged me to join the Executive Leadership Council (ELC) where I have had the opportunity to build deep connections with other Black corporate leaders over the years. My initial discomfort with the world he showed me has completely transformed. The world I didn't think I fit into has become a place where I belong. And no, I never again ate off someone else's plate without asking permission first.

Mike became an invaluable sponsor. And by seeing me, understanding what mattered to me, and leveraging his influence to aid me, he was responsible for some of my most important life and leadership transformations.

> * Think of a situation at work that made you uncomfortable. What did you learn from this experience?
>
> * What would you do differently next time you encounter this situation? What would you do the same?
>
> * What are some occasions where you might push yourself out of your comfort zone, and gain from it?
>
> * Remind yourself that you're moving toward growth. This reframing alone might help you move through uncomfortable moments.

Smart Risk-Taking

All growth, including learning to lead with meaning, involves not only discomfort but some degree of risk. In order to maximize your opportunities, I recommend learning how to take smart, calculated risks.

Risk management is a complex process that has fostered an entire industry. There are whole companies devoted to risk management and risk management frameworks. I've worked with some of the best, most sophisticated risk leaders and programs. What I will present here are some very basic concepts for managing risk, both personally and professionally. I want you to be armed with at least the fundamentals, as risk management is an important tool for leading with impact and growth.

Whenever we present a new idea, as you often do when you're leading with meaning, there's a risk that others will reject it. When I was leader of the corporate responsibility team, through our research we discovered that our guests had identified education as our top community investment priority. My team and I developed a strategic plan to refocus our community investment strategy and volunteerism. I wanted to do something we'd never done before—make a first-time multiyear philanthropic commitment to fund education initiatives. It was a bold billion-dollar plan.

The initial reaction from senior leadership was skepticism. There was a concern that the amount was too large and it projected too far into the future. What if we didn't have that revenue in five years? I could have acquiesced to their concerns, but I believed in the plan. Target could have an impact on the state of education in the United States and we would be addressing our guests' top priority.

I knew I needed to make the business case, and, truthfully, it was a bit daunting. I was going to have to talk to many teams and many stakeholders to get buy-in and support. We'd have to design and implement a whole new series of initiatives. But my belief in the potential payoff and impact of the education plan was strong. I was leading with meaning and willing to take the risk of others' pushback or rejection. In the end, the risk paid off. Target successfully invested $1 billion in education, and we leveraged our volunteers and business expertise to put more children on the path to graduation, readying them for college, life, and their careers.

Your Risk Appetite

Your risk appetite is the level of risk you are willing to accept or live with as you pursue your goals. It is a very individual thing. What are you willing to live with and live through? It's less important where you lie on the risk spectrum than that you understand your individual appetite for risk, or lack thereof.

Working as an entrepreneur often entails a very different risk appetite than working in the corporate world. Typically, your appetite for risk is higher if you choose the entrepreneurial track. Calling for the kind of societal change that Mrs. Coretta Scott King and Dr. King called for was also a high-risk endeavor. The upside to a high-risk appetite, as they say, is that higher risk often comes with a higher reward. Where does your risk appetite lie?

To simplify a bit, risks are often categorized into three buckets: financial, operational, and reputational. In an everyday example, think about the entrepreneur who wants to update their small business website. They're taking an *operational risk*. The changes they want or need to make might result in a glitch in the system—or even in the entire website going down. But if they need the upgrade and they've effectively planned how to mitigate that operational risk, they'll probably decide the new design or update is worth it. They may also be taking a *financial risk*. If the site goes down, they may not be able to sell goods or services during the update. Finally, if their site is down and their customers can't interact, they may take a *reputational* hit. People are often frustrated and disappointed when they expect to be able buy something or interact with an organization and they can't.

You may have a different threshold for different types of risks. For some the financial risk might be the key factor in their planning, while for others it might be the operational or reputational risk. A suicide prevention hotline might not be worried about the financial risk of being offline, but they might be very worried about the operational risk.

In reality, your threshold for risk is often a combination of all three. In another everyday example, a grocery store will think about the reputational, financial, and operational risk of adhering to food safety protocols, such as storing food properly and at the right temperature, because if they sell something unsafe, it's a pretty safe bet they'll see consequences on all three fronts: reputational, financial, and operational.

If you know the different kinds of risks you run and how much risk you're comfortable with—that is, if you know your risk appetite—it helps you manage accordingly and ensure the impact you want to make.

Personal Risk-Taking

From the get-go I've stressed that if you're leading with meaning you need to take a holistic approach to your life and career. You can't serve your purpose—or others—if you aren't taking care of yourself. So I'd be remiss if I didn't use this section on smart risk-taking to add a note on the importance of managing risk in not just your professional but also your personal life.

For some people taking risks is a rush. But for many others, there's stress involved in taking a leap. You want to do everything in your power to mitigate unforeseen bumps in the road, including having a financial plan for your future. Not planning for the unexpected can lead to stress and anxiety that take away your ability to lean into the other parts of pursuing your purpose or even cause you to take your eye off your larger purpose entirely. Can I get an amen?

Ann Fudge was instrumental to my learning process. Over the years, Ann has served as CEO and/or a C-suite leader for companies such as Young & Rubicam, Kraft, and General Mills. I first met her at a women's leadership forum hosted by the ELC in the early 2000s, where she opened my eyes to the necessity of having a holistic plan, including a financial plan for my future.

A what? As a young professional from humble roots with parents who worked multiple jobs, I didn't have any kind of plan. Many of us are first-generation wealth builders without a lot of knowledge on how to manage our finances. Which was exactly Ann's point. She saw financial freedom as a huge part of standing in our power. If we were financially solvent, we'd have more choice. If there was someone in our family we needed to be in service of or to help, we'd need the financial ability to make the choices that could help that person and still pay ourselves. We needed to cover our rent. And we needed to plan for the future.

I remember her saying, "I know you want to have fabulous outfits, a big house, and a beautiful car. And I don't want you to feel like you can't have those things—and more. But you should never live beyond your means. Pay yourself first." Ann wanted us to take smart, calculated risks, and to make the right choices, giving us the freedom to live our lives fully on our own terms.

Wow. That was the first time that anyone had broken down for me what it meant to live our lives with a holistic plan, including a plan for our finances. As I sat there listening to Ann, I realized that my husband, Bill, and I had elements of the plan, but there were huge gaps. We didn't have a financial planner and we certainly hadn't spent time establishing a financial strategy. We never had more than two nickels to rub together so it wasn't something that had even dawned on us.

I took Ann's words to heart that day. I was making more money than my parents did, but I had no idea how to make my money work for me. I listened—and not long after, Bill and I took action and slowly watched our two nickels grow into something bigger.

Along the way, Bill and I had to learn our appetite for risk. We knew we were comfortable with lower risk. We valued stability and economic mobility. Stability didn't mean we could stand still. We invested in a home that would increase in value over the years. We also saved for retirement by investment in our 401(k)s and in other investments that offered a consistent return, all while enjoying our lives in the moment and being there for our family and community when they needed us.

It's important to note that knowing your risk appetite doesn't 100 percent guarantee that your risk management will be successful. Life is life, and stuff happens. And it often happens when you least expect it. Layoffs occur, the sure thing falls through, your parents are sick and you need to take care of them. But if you're aware of your risk appetite, you can try to take steps to reduce the risk of your position at any particular life stage.

To take smart risks in your personal and professional life, you'll want to evaluate your or your organization's appetite for low, moderate, or high risk. Here are some basic tips to consider:

Determine your long-term objectives. Sit down and really think through your long-term goals and what exactly you need to get there. It's important to strategize and evaluate exactly what kind of risks you will need to take to achieve your goals. And it's worth keeping in mind that if your goal is growth you may need to take more risks than if your goal is maintenance or steady state. For example, if your goal is publicity or exposure, are you prepared for any reputational risks that you may face as part of making yourself or your business more visible? Or if your goal is the growth of your business through new product offerings, what kinds of operational risks might exist in your supply chain?

Assess your risk boundaries. Determine which risks you find acceptable, and which would be too risky for you at this time. For example, let's say you learn about the perfect home for your family or the perfect new office space for your organization. There might be operational risks if you need any kind of renovations to make it into a workable home or office space. There are also financial risks of taking the leap. Do the math. How do the mortgage payments compare to renting? What about that new computer or office equipment you might need or the loan payments you're still responsible for? Are you balancing your desire for economic mobility with economic reality?

Look at your current risk exposure. Based on the outcomes you'd like, should you be increasing your risk exposure and taking more risks? Or should you pull back and decrease your risk exposure? Or should you stay the same? Using the example above, if you have significant loans to pay off, or an investment you need to make in new inventory, you may not be in a position to take on the risk of a big mortgage. Similarly, if you've got a baby on the way, you may not be able to afford that new home. As much as you want and could use that new space, perhaps staying where you are for now and continuing to rent is the better solution.

Conversely, if you or your organization are relatively debt-free, perhaps you should be more risk-friendly than your initial impulse suggests. You may need that larger space to store your inventory as you grow.

Again, there is no right answer here. The point of articulating all this is to come to an understanding of your risk appetite and to manage your actions and plans accordingly; it's not to ensure that we all follow a cookie-cutter approach to risk-taking.

Finally, though we often overlook this: Doing nothing can be aggressively risky too. You may feel risk-averse, especially when it comes to putting your money in something unfamiliar, but the risk involved if you *don't* build your business or personal equity might be much worse than if you take the plunge. There are times when you simply have no choice but to act.

* Are you taking smart risks to further your growth? Is your risk appetite low, moderate, or high?

* Given your goals, what kinds of risks—regional, financial, and operational—might you be facing and what is your threshold for each type?

* Are you able to consider—and define—your risk boundaries related to career and/or personal risk?

* What is your current risk exposure, and what risks may be necessary in fulfilling your purpose?

* Which is better: failing to take a risk or acting on an opportunity available to you? You get to decide.

Scenario Planning

Getting uncomfortable and/or taking risks isn't something we can always manage or plan. Sometimes we are taken by surprise. Then comes the decision: What do we do? Learning to manage the uncomfortable situations we find ourselves in is another part of our growth.

Scenario planning is another basic tool you'll want in your toolbox when it comes to dealing with unexpected situations. The act of thinking through your various options allows you to pivot and yet stay on the path of your purpose. There is never just one way to do something. Often circumstances dictate that we have to adjust or adapt. If you're leading with meaning, you aren't going to give up just because the path you've chosen is no longer available. Rather, as circumstances change, you may need to find a different route. Scenario planning helps you think through future needs and situations and craft a variety of responses that you can call on in order to move forward. Scenario planning is a way of continuing to lead with impact.

Dealing with unexpected situations is something another important advisor of mine, Vernon Jordan, was accustomed to doing with warp speed. I was fortunate to be connected to Vernon by the late Jim Johnson, a former CEO, board director, and influential civic leader. Vernon served as the executive director of the United Negro College Fund and president and CEO of the National Urban League. He was also a prominent political and legal advisor to former president Bill Clinton and served on the board of directors for American Express, JCPenney, Dow Jones, Xerox, and Nabisco.

Because of Vernon's lived experience, he often had to operate in and navigate situations where he was the first one, the only one, or one of only a few Black people in the room. He shared many relevant and relatable experiences that were incredibly useful to me as I continued to navigate my roles inside the workplace and in everyday life. He taught me the importance of knowing how to fight back, without necessarily having to use my receipts. And he helped me learn how to think through various scenarios so that I always had a plan, even when the unexpected arose.

One such unexpected situation arose when I made an unintentional statement with my hair, of all things. It was a risk I'd never intended to take. Yet suddenly everyone was in an uproar. I had a decision to make. And I needed a forward plan.

For years, I had worn a very short corporate hairdo that was similar to styles worn by actresses Halle Berry and Angela Bassett in the late 1990s and early 2000s. For vacations, I would have my longtime hairstylist, Ms. Ruby, put in a set of braids for me. Braids were perfect for downtime and vacation travel as they were so much easier to maintain.

After one trip to Guatemala, Ms. Ruby and I didn't have time to undo the braids and return to my short do as we usually would have done. As a result, I showed up back in the office with my vacation braids intact. The reaction shocked me.

I never could have imagined the turmoil that one set of braids would bring. I got quizzical looks and curious questions from folks internally and externally. Some people even had the nerve to touch my braids without my permission (unfortunately, a common experience for many Black women). People were whispering, "Girl, are you about to get fired?" or "Are you going to get in trouble?" Others asked if I was leaving the company, because they couldn't believe a C-suite leader who reported to the CEO could wear braids in the office. Those assumptions alone spoke volumes. At the same time, I was also struck by the leaders—particularly the Black leaders—who said they were inspired seeing an executive in a natural hairstyle. It wasn't my intention to make a statement, yet I had made one nonetheless.

Adding to the upset, I was suddenly feeling attached to these braids that I had never meant to wear back to work. The more questions I got, the more I started to feel like this "minor" incident actually spoke to much larger issues, important issues that I cared about. Though the incident took place in 2015, the prevalence of hair discrimination in the workplace and in schools eventually led to the CROWN (Create a Respectful and Open World for Natural Hair) Act, which didn't pass the Senate but did prompt a number of states to pass legislation prohibiting discrimination based on hairstyle and hair texture.

When I told Vernon about the reactions, he shared his perspective. He told me he was always an advocate for being yourself—as long as your choices didn't discount your performance or become a distraction. And if your choices did become a distraction, you still needed to be able to handle your business—and the pressure. In this case, Vernon used Ursula Burns as an example. She was a strong and capable leader who became CEO of Xerox and the first Black female CEO of a Fortune 500 company. And she sported a close-cropped short natural hairstyle, which was outside of the norm.

Vernon wasn't saying I couldn't succeed with braids, he only wanted me to understand that my choice could come with consequences. He told me that it could impact opportunities that came my way. And he reminded me that we were still dealing with unconscious and conscious bias. He told me, "I got you"—but I needed to have my eyes wide open.

Vernon didn't want me to be paranoid or paralyzed by the potential risks. He just wanted me to thoughtfully play out the scenarios, like we'd done with so many issues over the years.

Scenario planning, like calculating one's risk appetite, is a way of managing risk or discomfort, especially as we seek to change and grow. When we scenario plan, we ask a series of questions about possible future outcomes in order to consider the various alternatives in play. Essentially, you are modeling various situations that can impact your business or yourself.

Vernon was by nature a scenario planner. So I can't say it came as much of a surprise when he suggested that we approach the question of what to do about my hair the same way we approached any scenario I was struggling to resolve, and model the various possible outcomes of sticking with my new braids.

Like any good scenario plan, the first step was to construct a decision tree.

To construct a decision tree you write down each possible decision. Then articulate what would happen if you made that decision. What scenario arises? And what possible outcome is the result? You repeat the process for as many possible decisions as you could make.

In the case of my hair, what would happen if I kept the braids? On the other hand, if I went back to my short do, what scenario would arise from that? And what possible outcome could result?

As you make a tree of the possible decisions, the resulting scenarios, and the resulting outcomes, you get a fuller picture of how each decision will play out, enabling you to make the best decision possible.

Alternatively, scenario planning can take the form of a flow chart:

- **What could happen?** This is where you think about all the possible futures.

- **What is most likely to happen?** Here is where you model out the most likely future.

- **What do you want to happen?** Here is where you look at your most desired outcome.

There are many ways to scenario plan. You may also look at factors that will affect the scenario. Your personal beliefs and attitudes are important, especially when it comes to any kind of risky behavior, whether it's investing in stocks, moving jobs, or braving public opinion. Your beliefs matter.

In the case of my hair, we didn't literally draw flow charts! But we did examine the possible outcomes of each decision—to keep or not to keep. We looked at the possible futures: My braids might be positively perceived. Or they might be negatively perceived. Initially, I wasn't totally sure which was most likely—or even what I wanted. I then went to my decision tree: If my braids were positively perceived, would I want to keep them intact? And if my braids were negatively perceived, would I fight it? Or would I go back to my short, cropped hairstyle?

I'd been an external spokesperson at Target for a number of years. And my appearance at the time mattered. Vernon wanted to know how uncomfortable I was willing to get.

"That's a really hard question," I said. I hadn't been planning to make a grand statement. The whole thing was a result of a post-travel rush!

Ultimately, the response to my braids became the deal-breaker. I couldn't believe the number of comments that I got, both inside and outside of Target. When people told me they assumed I was leaving the company, it only strengthened my resolve to keep my hair the way it was. Braids in the workplace should be normalized; we shouldn't be ostracized over a hairstyle. That others saw themselves in the struggle encouraged me to keep the new look. As I've mentioned, our own beliefs and attitudes matter.

Wearing braids doesn't work out for everybody. And you don't need to fall on your sword for everything. Everything isn't a lunch counter. If it's not strategic, if it's not wise, you need to ask yourself: Do you want to win the battle or the war? As I like to say, keep the main thing the main thing.

Going back to my scenario planning, though, I felt confident that after a twenty-five-plus-year career, I had the track record and that my appearance wouldn't become more important than my impact. I felt that my desired outcome, a positive response, would also be the most likely one: My environment would accept my braids. They did. And I still have the braids today.

Keeping my braids kept me on a path that supported my purpose and helped me lead with meaning. The world had changed, my options had changed, and reaffirming my choice of a natural hairstyle was aligned with my purpose of opening opportunities for others; I wanted others to be able to make the choice that was right for them.

- Take a situation that you know involves risk and try to scenario plan it out.

- What happens if you make Decision number one? Decision number two?

- What are the possible outcomes? What's the likely outcome? What's the desired outcome?

- What decisions or actions could you take to increase the odds of getting your desired outcome?

Take Relationship Risks

Ultimately every risk we take is balanced against the possible opportunity that might result. And though I encourage planning and analysis, there are times when you have to go with your gut. This is especially true when it comes to some of our most important risks—forming relationships. Getting to know people with whom you, at least initially, seem to have nothing in common can feel stressful. It's also a terrific way to grow.

When I moved to Minneapolis in 1999, I was doing community relations work for the department store division, which included

Dayton's, Hudson's, and Marshall Field's. A year later, I took on responsibility for the company's foundation, which was transitioning, along with the corporation, from Dayton-Hudson to Target.

The newly named foundation would carry forward the company's legacy of philanthropic commitment—giving 5 percent of profits to the communities we served. Decades before corporate social responsibility became mainstream, the Dayton family embedded community giving into the DNA of Dayton's department stores, establishing a tradition of corporate responsibility that has been passed down from generation to generation.

When the Target Foundation became a core part of my role, the weight of this new responsibility was heavy. I was now in a position to carry on the generational values and legacy of impact created by the Dayton family. I was both honored and nervous to be leading the foundation at the same time that the Target brand was moving front and center on Wall Street and across America. Finding myself in a visible role in a year of big milestones for the company was surprising, exciting, and a little bit frightening—and my top priority was making sure that the Dayton family felt honored and included throughout the rebranding process.

As I was settling into my new role, I received a note from Mr. Bruce Dayton, one of the founders of the company:

Dear Ms. Ward,

Congratulations! The position of head of Target foundation offers you a great challenge and a great opportunity. Over the recent years, the foundation has continued to improve its effectiveness through the involvement of increasing numbers within the corporation. With enlarged amounts available, you have the opportunity to seek

some of the solutions which are so urgent in our cities.
Good luck in your exciting new role.

> Sincerely yours,
> Bruce B. Dayton

He also included a leadership book with the letter—*and* he copied Bob Ulrich, then CEO, on his correspondence. As a newcomer to Minneapolis and a new mid-level leader, I was blown away. Years later, I realized that Mr. Bruce did this kind of outreach for all new hires in positions that were meaningful to him. But at the time, it simply felt like what it was: an amazing recognition—of me, of my new role, and of the values of the company I was working for.

I then did something that not everyone does anymore but which has always served me well: I wrote him back. In twenty-first-century life, many people shrug off correspondence, especially physical correspondence. Between email, texts, and social media DMs, there's an avalanche of material in our inboxes. But if someone you admire who has the power to change your life sends you even a pro forma letter, answer them. After all, you never know what will come of it. And sometimes, as with Mr. Bruce and me, much more happens than you ever anticipated.

Shortly after I sent my reply, I got a call from his team inviting me to join him at the Minneapolis Club. I'll admit, it was intimidating. I'd answered his note because my momma had taught me good manners. But I never thought my reply would lead to a further connection. My first thought was, "Uh-oh. He's inviting me to the old, rich white men's club to make sure that I don't mess up the family legacy." I assumed I would get schooled and lectured, and we'd never connect again. Still, I nervously accepted the invitation. Again, you never know where a chance meeting will lead.

When I arrived at the Minneapolis Club, I was immediately overwhelmed. I didn't even know that such places existed! Membership was by "invitation or referral," so no wonder I didn't know. The club is located downtown in a historic 1907 building. In 2000, it was dimly lit and ornately decorated with dark oak and silver and gold chandeliers throughout.

That day, it was so quiet you could hear a church mouse. I felt like every step I took up the stairs was announcing my arrival. My mind started pinging around thoughts like "Am I allowed in here?" and "Do they even let Black people in?" As I looked around the room, that old song from *Sesame Street* started looping in my head: "*One of these things is not like the other . . .*"

Fortunately, my nervousness didn't have much time to escalate, because as soon as Bruce Dayton walked into the club, his demeanor set me at ease. His presence was just as warm and inviting as his letter. He shared that he wanted to be a resource for me, and he suggested that we might discover opportunities to learn from one another. He seemed genuinely focused on helping me learn and grow. And, as it turned out, we had a wonderful conversation filled with humanity.

Things quickly got more personal. I shared with him that moving to Minnesota had been professionally wonderful, but personally difficult—and I could see that he was open and curious. He was seeking to understand. Feeling more comfortable, I decided to broach a personal question as well: I asked him what it was like not to be running the family business anymore. He seemed to appreciate my genuine interest in him, and to my surprise, he answered forthrightly.

He said that initially, at least, it was hard not to be part of the day-to-day. Over time, however, it became easier, especially when he saw the legacy he'd left, when he saw the business grow as the result of others investing their time and energy in it as he once did.

It was then that I began to understand that this meeting wasn't about him formulating a strategy or critiquing me, as I'd anticipated. Nor was he there to second-guess me or the company or to try to take on a role that wasn't his to take. He did have some expectations, but they boiled down to this: that I would do the work wisely, and that I would do it in my own way. He made it clear that he was there to support. He went on to say that, if I were open to it, we could meet on a regular basis at the club. I was humbled by and grateful for his gracious offer.

As we got to know each other better, built trust, and deepened our relationship, I started to call him "Mr. Bruce." From our first meeting in 2000 until his death in 2015, Mr. Bruce and I would meet at least once a year at the Minneapolis Club, until his health waned, when we began to meet at his home.

In between our meetings, we would talk on the phone or he'd send me notes. While he was always very interested in talking about the business and being in the know about Target's evolution, Mr. Bruce and I would also talk about topics you weren't supposed to discuss—from politics to religion to race relations to the environment. Sometimes I wondered if I was overstepping by engaging in these talks, but I stayed focused on listening, learning, and sharing. There was a great deal of reciprocity. He wasn't just passing down his wisdom from on high. I was keeping him updated with all the new technology. I would bring my iPad over and show him how I used it at work and in my everyday life. He got a big kick out of it. We were learning from each other, just as he had suggested from the beginning.

I'm often asked how I initially formed my relationships with supporters such as Mr. Bruce. There's definitely some luck involved. But as you can probably glean from this story, there are also some lessons to take to heart. It's important to always follow up, even when you don't expect anything to come from it. Be brave and put yourself in a position where you are visible to those who have the power to make a difference. And again, be open to the possibility that even those who are very different from you are interested, interesting, and might even be people with whom you have things in common. It's easy to run from relationships with the powerful. I understand that it's an intimidating situation when our idols, or those who have already achieved a great deal, come into our orbit. Yet they can be as interested in you as you are in them. You both have things to teach each other. Remember what we discussed in chapter 1: Bet on and believe in you. They are. Run toward those opportunities.

Finally, remember that we all share a common humanity. The more you learn to treat others, whoever they are, with the respect, good humor, and dignity we all want to be accorded, the better you'll become at forging relationships, no matter how much success the person across the table has had.

Leaders pursue opportunities even when there are risks involved. Remember that it is always up to you: Ultimately, it's your choice and your power. Determine your risk appetite and scenario plan, then make the decision that best fits you. It doesn't need to be the decision anyone else would have made; it just needs to be yours.

Always move forward to growth. You will come to believe that you are worthy of all the spaces you enter. It's an incredibly important first step in seeing that you belong. Each time, you start to believe that. And the next time, you believe it more. When you are willing to make yourself uncomfortable, you will see that on the other side of risk is opportunity. When you are leading with meaning, you can't be afraid to take smart risks. You'll quickly find that by taking some calculated risks your growth and impact will substantially increase.

PS from Laysha

Evaluating your risk appetite and using scenario planning can help you make informed decisions about the steps you want to take to lead with meaning. But remember, they are tools to guide you. Your values come first. This is your life and leadership learning journey. Don't just go through life, grow through life.

CHAPTER SIX

Listen, Debate, Negotiate

We have two ears and one mouth so that we
can listen twice as much as we speak.

—UNKNOWN

When I was a little girl back in Indiana, my kindergarten teacher once shared with my mom and dad that I was "bright, bossy, and talked too much." This was before we moved to my new school, where I was much shyer. And while my teacher's feedback wasn't entirely true, it wasn't entirely inaccurate either. Still, it was a negative-sounding characterization of traits that in a boy would most likely be seen as budding leadership skills. Surely it was a good thing to be bright, willing to take charge, and highly verbal? I was a communicator!

Effective communication is a complex topic, and I've learned a great deal since my kindergarten teacher called me "chatty." In time, however, I've come to understand that being highly verbal, bright, and willing to take charge are necessary, but not sufficient, skills for great communication. In fact, communication is only in part about speech. What the most effective communicators do well is engage others. They are active listeners, they know how to foster healthy debate, and they are patient negotiators. Engagement is essential to a strong leader's success.

From my earliest roles in our stores to my final role as strategic advisor at Target, I spent a great deal of time listening, debating, and negotiating solutions with stakeholders, who ranged from business, nonprofit, and community leaders to elected officials, guests (Target customers), and team members (Target employees). In my board and community roles, I am in constant contact with a wide range of people from all walks of life who represent a wide array of points of view. Over the years, I've learned to get very good at communicating with people with whom I might initially have little in common. On my journey, I've picked up some useful tips. Not only will learning to effectively listen, debate, and negotiate make you a better communicator, but treating people with respect and dignity is one of the hallmarks of leading with meaning.

Listen

Weak listening skills are a common challenge for leaders. Most people know they should be doing a better job. But improving our listening skills isn't as easy as it sounds. It can be tough to sit there, silent, truly soaking in another's point of view, especially if you're used to framing the discussion and/or to using meetings to ensure that *your* voice is heard.

Listening is essential in building relationships, whether personal or professional. Michael Hyter describes it this way, "Listening—and truly hearing—is the essence of building familiarity and trust." Truly hearing another, or active listening, is how you uncover the other person's truth. And when you know their truth, you can better understand, support, empathize, and partner with them. This is what listening to learn and understand is all about—and it's increasingly important for leaders in today's evolving hybrid workplace and world. It's also crucial for leading with meaning.

As part of a developmental series with my peers several years ago, I learned about three types of listening:

- **Listening to win.** This is when there's a decision being made, and you're listening to figure out how you can sway the audience to adopt your solution.

- **Listening to fix.** This type of listening happens when there's a problem to solve and you're listening just long enough to offer a solution.

- **Listening to learn and understand.** This is when you approach a conversation from a place of openness and curiosity. You're less likely to interrupt and more likely to ask questions.

Which type of listening do you do?

Many of us would protest that we don't simply listen to win—or to fix! Yet we all do it. Sometimes it's because you're under pressure, time is short, and you've already made up your mind. You want quick agreement, not extended discussion. Sometimes it's because you fear hearing what others have to say. Perhaps you feel insecure in your own position, and in the moment, you want support. Perhaps you genuinely believe you already know the best answer and just want to fix the problem.

There's always that temptation to engage in selective listening, and to confirm your own presuppositions. The problem with selective listening, or filtering what you hear through your own bias, is that it prevents you from actively hearing the full extent of what the other speaker is trying to communicate. You will then distort the facts to fit your own solution. In the worst-case scenario, the problem will not be solved. In the best-case scenario, opportunities will be left on the table.

This does not have to be the case.

Good listening is good communication. It helps you maintain relationships, personally and professionally, and become a much more skilled problem-solver. Here are some best practices to keep in mind.

Listening Is a Path to Learning

When I listen to learn or understand, I actively try to retain the new information I hear and digest it. By engaging with what I'm hearing, I am much better equipped for the conversation I am in, and I gain insights that help with future conversations. This kind of informational listening is crucial to problem-solving. It's also just good communication.

When I was being coached by Teresa Lyons-Hegdahl, who had been my speech coach since my early days at Target, on making speeches and presentations, we discussed what makes a superior podcast interviewer. I, like the good student, had prepared a list of questions to ask my celebrity guests. Teresa pointed out, however, that the best conversations do not always hew to the prepared questions, they take off from them and go in unexpected directions. She encouraged me to free myself from a strict list and go wherever the conversation took us. This made me slightly nervous as it meant I would really have to listen intently to every response so as to know where I should go next. I might even have to skip around; a guest's response might correspond to something I intended to ask much later. Question six might have to become question two. But the result was a richer, deeper, genuine connection with my interviewee. I was genuinely learning from them as we went, and it made for some incredible podcasts. Listening to learn directly from others ensures you are present and truly absorbing others' insights and points of view.

Listening Is Empathetic

The best listeners not only acknowledge others, they try to put themselves in their shoes, so that they can understand their experience. Putting yourself in others' shoes is key to civil discourse. It's good people skills. And it's good leadership.

Sondra Samuels is the CEO and president of the Northside Achievement Zone (NAZ), a group in Minneapolis that focuses on addressing multigenerational poverty. I've been involved with the organization for years, and though there are lot of organizations that try to tackle this complex, difficult issue, Sondra's approach stands out. She carefully listens to the children and families she's trying to help, putting herself in their shoes—their issues are her issues. She also lives in the neighborhood, something few other leaders would do, calling herself a proud Northsider. Through this proximity, she experiences the same day-to-day challenges faced by the people she's committed to help. Aided by her empathetic listening, she leads NAZ and collaborates with their partner organizations with enormous humanity, integrity, and impact. She's a force of nature and goodness. Sondra leads with meaning.

Listening Is Critical

Critical listening is often the last stage of decision-making—and a crucial leadership skill. When you listen critically you are actively trying to hear and understand what others say. You have used informational listening to gather the facts and empathetic listening to put yourself in another's shoes. You then need to analyze and evaluate all the facts you have gathered against the bigger picture to determine the best resolution.

The more complex the issue, the more essential it becomes to use critical listening to make your decision. You may not be able to resolve certain complex issues to everyone's satisfaction, but if you've considered the various factors and evaluated them in light of the bigger picture, you will sit comfortably with your decision. I learned this the hard way with an especially challenging situation that Target faced.

I was asked to co-lead an internal effort to assess whether we should consistently enforce Target's no-solicitation policy. A growing number of organizations were attempting to solicit donations, sell goods, or distribute promotional materials at our stores—and the policy was being inconsistently applied. We were receiving increasing guest complaints that the organizations' solicitations were detracting from the guest experience we were working hard to create. And our teams were being placed in awkward positions in their local communities. Our senior leaders had differing views about how hard and fast we should apply the no-solicitation policy.

We needed to listen critically to our leaders' different views, with the goal of effectively evaluating the situation and recommending a course of action. Our team spent months discussing, debating, and vetting our potential recommendations with teams across the company and outside experts. We did a situational analysis and assessed the reputational, operational, and financial impact of the policy. Ultimately, we presented our recommendation back to the senior leadership team and they decided to reinforce the no-solicitation policy.

Despite our critical listening and sound analysis, our "no-solicitation" decision quickly got messy and controversial, with protests and negative media coverage. Things got even worse for me when the top executive of a prominent nonprofit organization that was affected by Target's decision—and was very unhappy about it—reached out to our CEO, Bob Ulrich. This leader very mistakenly assumed that the decision had been made solely by me, and he recommended, in a long letter, that I be terminated immediately. Bob called me to his office and tossed the letter across the table to me. When I read it, my body went hot with anger and then quickly turned cold with fear.

As I read the letter, I was thinking, "Are you kidding me? Give me a break!" I'd like to pretend that I was powerful enough to have been the sole decision-maker here, but in reality, very few decisions in corporate America rest solely on one person. Even though I knew I wasn't deserving of all the backlash, I was scared that I might end up taking the fall for Target's decision and get fired.

But then Bob spoke, and I'll never forget his words. He said, "Laysha, you might get fired someday, but it won't be for this." His gruff and stoic reassurance calmed me down immediately. He knew the hard work that we'd put in to ensure alignment with relevant teams across the company, and he clearly wasn't going to let a moment of bad PR derail a good—and well-considered—decision for the brand. I was relieved that he had my back. And equally relieved that our analysis, evaluation, and final recommendation had been sound. The critical listening we'd done had served Target well and Bob's unwavering support for our ultimate decision confirmed that.

No matter what decision you're making in business, you'll likely always have supporters and detractors. It's hard to be free from controversy. But if you have done the listening work and used it to inform your decision, you will be better prepared for whatever comes. I am constantly practicing my listening skills.

Listening Requires Practice

Good listening requires patience and discipline. I am still a talker. But over the years, I have learned to be patient and hold back when I am eager to say something. And the more I have held back, the deeper and more open my conversations have become. Like any skill, listening needs to be practiced. Am I a perfect listener? Not even close. But I am better than I was in elementary school—and better today than I was yesterday.

When Zoom came into our lives, many of us felt like we had to practice what it meant to be a good listener all over again. Being on Zoom for hours required me to build a different muscle around listening—when to hold back, when to jump in—it's a whole different rhythm and practice. I needed to be attentive, not zone out, and be able to track who on the screen was talking, especially when there are literally a thousand people in the Zoom room. I used to affirm I was listening with a nod; now I was no longer sure anyone could even see my nod.

With Zoom, it's helpful to have rules of engagement and discuss them up front. I suggest clarifying from the start whether people should raise their virtual hands and/or put their questions and comments in the chat to effectively listen and engage.

On Zoom, it can also be hard to know if you're engaging or interrupting. Stating the rules can help everyone relax and focus on the speaker, without cutting off the listeners' ability to participate. We don't get a pass on being an effective and engaged listener just because we are on Zoom. And it's always a valuable exercise, no matter the medium or the forum, to practice our listening skills.

Here are some additional best practices to try to truly listen to others:

- **Start with a question.** Rather than leading with a statement, ask a question. Instead of saying, "I think," begin a discussion by asking others what they think.

- **Give others a chance to share before you speak.** At a team meeting, start a discussion by going around the table and getting everyone else's thoughts. Speak only once others have weighed in.

- **Don't interrupt.** Take a beat. Breathe. Listen to what your counterpart is trying to get across.

- **WAIT.** This is one of my favorites. WAIT is an acronym that stands for "Why am I talking?" Does whatever you're about to say need to be said? Does it need to be said by you? Does it need to be said now? Remember, you don't have to contribute just to contribute. It's always worth asking yourself these questions before launching in.

- Think of a recent discussion you engaged in at work or with a friend or family member.

- What was the problem you were trying to solve?

- Did you actively listen to your discussion partner(s)' perspective and suggestions? Or did you listen to win or to fix?

- Be honest. If you did actively listen, how did you actively listen?

- If you were listening to learn, what did you learn?

- If you were listening with empathy, what did you dis-cover by stepping into their shoes?

- If you engaged in critical listening, how did it help you come up with the best solution?

- I know it's unlikely you can revisit the subject with your discussion partner, but if you didn't use the various forms of listening at the time, do it as a thought exercise.

- What might have you learned or how would the outcome have changed if you had used all the forms of listening?

- Try to practice the various forms of listening in your next discussion.

A Personal Note on Speaking, Listening, and Sharing Oneself

I mentioned in the introduction that I would be combining advice on how to work on your leadership skills with advice on how to work on yourself. This is one of those holistic learning moments. Because as much as everything we've discussed about listening is true, I've also learned the hard way that even if you've finely honed your listening skills, there are occasions where listening only works and helps you foster genuine exchange if you are willing to do some self-work, let your guard down, and share yourself. In any real exchange, you need to be willing to open up. Or others will stay closed too. Trust goes both ways. And trust, shared empathy, and sharing oneself are some-times what's required in a situation where you hope to genuinely communicate. I had many discussions with Dr. Michael Lomax on this topic. And because what came out of those talks was such a key lesson for me, I want to share it with you.

I first met Dr. Michael Lomax more than twenty years ago. At the time, I was managing Target's relationship with the United Negro College Fund (UNCF), and Dr. Lomax was the president and CEO. When we started working together, I was very focused on delivering results, performing at the highest level, protecting the Target brand, and proving that I deserved to be in that leadership position. I also felt a deep commitment to UNCF. So I was demanding, of myself and others—and I know for a fact that I was getting on Dr. Lomax's nerves. I can look back now and see that I just wanted the world to know that I deserved to be there. That I wasn't a token hire. Every time I showed up, I wanted to prove I belonged in the room and could deliver results.

In the beginning, I don't think Dr. Lomax liked me. But what drew us together—and ultimately made him one of my life's touchstones—is that he could relate to me. We had our beefs and challenges—but he saw me. He knew the struggle. He knew I was being tough on him because I was being tough on myself.

Fast-forward to 2023, decades into our relationship. Dr. Lomax called to check on my well-being several weeks after my father passed. During our conversation, I told him I was writing a book. He asked if I would be including a section on sharing oneself. It was a topic that we'd talked about over the years. He said, "Laysha, when I first met you, you were very guarded. Given the positions you had been in and the spotlight that had been on you, I understood it. You've often had no choice but to protect yourself fiercely.

"I also saw your journey to let go of that armor or self-protectiveness, a transformation in which you increasingly opened yourself up to others, becoming more relatable in the process. I hope you'll be discussing the importance of sharing yourself in the book, as it could be a valuable lesson to pass on."

The more we talked, the more I was reminded about the heavy armor I had carried for most of my life. I knew writing a book meant removing a layer or two and revealing more of myself, but hearing it from Dr. Lomax really made it sink in.

He was right—in the past, I'd worn my armor like a second skin. When I first met Dr. Lomax, I had my guard up. Over the years, I slowly but surely learned that I could trust him and let him see the chinks in my armor. He told me, in more than one vulnerable moment over the years, that he could see that I was a very caring person and that when I shared my truths, that more open and approachable side of me came bursting through. He was right. Opening up to others, I'd learned, made me an even better colleague and leader.

Even back in the days when I was less open, I was aware that my guarded tendencies were often misinterpreted as an inability to effectively listen and communicate. Which is how I came up with a system of signals to remind me to speak, listen, and share more of myself. When I first moved to Minneapolis from Chicago, I got feedback that my approach was too dominating and direct. A colleague of mine, Laura Sandall, had moved to Minneapolis from Chicago before I did—and had also been told to stop being a bull in a china shop. She was hearing that the directness that had served her well in Chicago wasn't as appreciated in Minneapolis. So we had that in common.

But there were some clear distinctions in the feedback we were getting, too. She was being told that she talked too much and needed to be a better listener—and that she was "oversharing" information.

My feedback was that I didn't share enough. That I was both too direct and too "guarded," which sounds like a contradiction, but is more common feedback than you think. When we feel like we're in an environment where we don't feel a strong sense of trust, our armor goes on, and though we may still try to be direct and make ourselves heard, we aren't always contributing to an environment of mutual sharing and openness. In this context, others may misinterpret our directness as a criticism, not an offering, and even fail to see us a team player, which was the feedback I was getting.

Laura and I were peers, so she was an ideal buddy to help me read the room and figure out how to respond when what I was saying and how I was saying it was far from Minnesota Nice. The truth was some of this was an issue of me needing to be more open, but some of it was a cultural and style difference over how direct to be, and some of it was just me trying to make myself heard and respected in a new environment.

Laura and I established a set of subtle signs to alert me when I needed to perhaps back off a bit and listen to others. We called it the Carol Burnett ear tug as the primary signal for me to monitor my tone, to listen more, and to maybe share more of myself. In one instance, I was so wrapped up in my point of view that I missed the signal. But I didn't miss Laura's second attempt, when she activated our emergency signal: *The Thinker* by Rodin. She placed her elbow under her chin with her head slightly down just like the famous sculpture. I knew then that I had to pause and soften my approach a bit. I didn't need to stop speaking, but I did need to adapt my approach and open up so that others felt like their perspective was being heard as well.

For some this might be a triggering conversation, so let me be clear: I am not advising you to make yourself small. Women, in particular, are often told that they're being difficult or too aggressive if they speak up too much. I don't want you to feel silenced. But you do need to find a way of communicating where you can be both direct and yet open to others, where you and others can feel respected and heard. Speak, listen, and share. If you are doing all three, you will be heard and seen as a team player.

Being more open and vulnerable is a journey I am still on, though I have come a long way over the past twenty-five years. The work I've done has made me a better listener, a better colleague, and a better communicator.

Healthy Debate

Over the years, I have learned how to be more relatable by seeking to understand other people's stories and lived experiences by listening. This has helped me connect with people in a way that minimizes polarization and discord and creates an authentic way to be in community—engaging in civil debate, even when we disagree with each other.

Healthy debate is having the courage to give voice to divergent points of view. We're often so conflict-averse that we fear "going there." "What if an explosion results?" we worry. We then use that concern to rationalize staying silent. We remain quiet and avoid conflict. But we need to air conflicting perspectives so that we can develop the right solutions.

I know, civil debate feels impossible these days. But that's precisely why it's so important that we institute good practices. Healthy debate is possible. And crucial for leading with meaning.

The key is to put in place some ground rules when we have these discussions. Ground rules are what allow divergent voices to be heard and healthy debate to flourish. Here are my rules:

Make sure you know what problem you are trying to solve. Why are you here? What are you trying to accomplish? Are you all agreed or aligned on the destination? A failure to be aligned on the problem you are trying to solve is often the quickest way to derail a discussion. Clarity on goals helps you keep things focused.

It's easy to get excited about our purpose and our ideas, believe me, I know. Yet it's important to remember that leading with meaning is not all about you—or the plan you've already decided on. It's about identifying the problem you want to solve, the audience you want to impact, and the opportunity you're trying to unlock. These are all things that should be helping you focus the discussion.

Humanize the others in the room. Even five minutes of an icebreaker or a personal connection will help you move through the inevitable conflict that will arise in a meeting. Find something that can help you connect, like figuring out what people love to do in their off time. If you're a sports person, you might connect over your favorite team. Musical artists can be a potential link. Do you share a connection on social media? You can even start a meeting with a structured question for everyone to answer, such as identifying an artifact they own that means something to them. Maybe it's a brightly colored mug that says "Love," a lucky baseball cap, or a painted rock that proclaims, "It's OK not to be OK." (I have a collection of painted rocks with many sayings like these!) Any insight we get into who we are helps us to see each other as fellow humans, not adversaries.

Ask questions, but do so with genuine curiosity and positive intent. It's always good to start by explaining *why* you are asking questions.

State up front that you are asking because you're seeking to understand others' perspective on issues. Be clear that you are suspending judgment. Don't just ask questions that serve your own agenda. Practice your good listening skills. Don't come into a discussion with the intent to listen to win or to listen to fix. Be genuinely curious about others' points of view and experiences. Also, be sure that your tone and your body language conveys your positive intent. A series of rapid-fire questions can shut people down. If you're crossing your arms or rolling your eyes or giving a heavy sigh, people will pick up on it, even if it was inadvertent on your part. Look, we all get tired or frustrated in meetings, but the more we can stay curious and positive in our questioning, the healthier the debate remains.

Have the courage and conviction to honor your truth, though not at the expense of others. Avoid generalizing, stereotyping, speaking hypothetically, and instead be true to your own personality, spirit, values, and experiences. Listen first and then speak to your own experience. Don't silence others. But also don't silence yourself. We all need to hear each other's perspectives.

I remember a meeting early in my career, when I was also in school, getting my master's degree from the University of Chicago. I was collaborating with a group of cross-sector leaders for a class project, and we started talking about preschool programs as a pathway to developing life and career skills. The goal of the project was to develop more effective policies and programs for the kids and families in Head Start.

A member of our group threw shade at Head Start by saying that "those people in that program" are "never going to be ready for the future workforce." They went on to further characterize the people and the program as deficit-based as opposed to asset-based. The comments were dismissive—and totally disconnected from the dignity, humanity, and potential of the individuals and community. It was hard for me to hear, but I forced myself to listen to this perspective that differed from my own.

As I was listening, I saw the faces of the kids, families, and teachers in my Head Start program back in Indiana who were taking steps toward a better life. I felt a responsibility to represent their voices. The room was loud and noisy, but I had a seat at the table, and so I said, "I went to Head Start."

Silence.

And then the real conversation began.

That only happened because I had the patience and discipline to hear what was being said in the room, which allowed me to understand and then fix a misrepresentation. I honored their perspective, but I also did not stay silent about my own experiences, experiences that would directly inform the problem we were trying to solve! I honored my truth—and our proposed policies and solutions were better informed as a result.

Call out people's behaviors, expressions, or even silences in order to call them in. People may not be being intentionally rude. Their scrunched-up face or lack of contribution to the conversation may indicate that they are processing or wrestling with something in the moment. You call people out not to blame and shame, but to call them in. Maybe there's a story or insight in that sigh or side-eye that could be a valuable lesson for the team. It's also important to recognize that sometimes people simply need more time to process something. Whatever they are thinking and feeling in the moment, they need that time to reflect on it before they respond. In that case, acknowledge their processing and assure them that you can always circle back.

These ground rules aren't dictates. They are guidelines that encourage mutual respect, collegiality, and genuine engagement. Note that there are times when you simply can't follow the rules. During the pandemic, Target had to accelerate the timeline for decision-making. We were forced to make hundreds of decisions a day. And to do so in a context where life and death were literally at stake. We did try to honor our ground rules and employ the various kinds of listening, but in-depth explorations of each other's points of view are extremely difficult in a crisis moment. In some cases, as a leadership team, we broke into smaller working groups. Not everybody needed to weigh in on every decision. A decision such as requiring customers and employees to wear masks in the store generated plenty of discussion, some of it tense. Our goal was to always follow the science and keep our guests' and teams' safety paramount, but given the rapidly changing environment and guidance, the path for doing so wasn't always crystal clear. We still had to make a call. And often do it quickly.

The experience reinforced for me that my boss at the time, Brian Cornell, was one of the best leaders in times of disruption and crisis that I've ever worked with. He is calm, provides clarity, is an excellent communicator, and he's decisive. He wasn't paralyzed by the crisis; he was able to quickly mobilize the team and make effective decisions. And he honored the ground rules up to the point where the decisions were unprecedented and the rules hadn't been written yet.

Not all leaders will maintain all the rules or even civility in every moment. But here is where your ability to surround yourself with a great team matters. If you have created a team with a diverse set of capabilities and shared goals, somebody else can pick up wherever and whenever you aren't able to continue. Just because you are the most senior in the room doesn't mean that you have to be the one who processes everything in the moment. Great leaders are humans too.

Learning to listen and follow the ground rules helps ensure healthy debate. And the healthier the debate, the easier it is to make hard choices. I often tell the story of how in 1996, long before there was pressure from outside forces to not sell cigarettes, Target decided to cease carrying tobacco products in its stores. It was the first large retail chain to do so. To help you understand how revolutionary this was at the time, Walmart didn't stop selling cigarettes in the majority of its stores until 2022, twenty-six years after Target did, and even then, some of its stores continued to sell cigarettes. CVS removed cigarettes in 2014. To stop selling cigarettes in 1996 wasn't just a bold decision; it was a jaw-dropping one. Why would Target give up $15.8 billion in sales?

Also, here's the kicker. At the time, several of the people on the executive committee who made this decision were *heavy smokers*. Now, I wasn't in the boardroom, but I knew some of the players. I can't imagine they all loved making the choice to drop an item they were personally so attached to. Many of the people in that room had a dog in the fight. And as we discussed with listening to win and listening to fix, personal preferences can quickly skew our decisions.

Yet the executive committee managed to have a healthy debate on the issue. I can't tell you that they followed all the ground rules. But by all accounts, they asked a lot of questions and did a lot of listening. Ultimately, they came up with the surprising conclusion to get out of the cigarette business. There were a lot of factors involved. But they followed the first rule of knowing what the problem was they were trying to solve. And that helped them keep their eye on the ball.

They started by considering the various factors. Target's values were to be aligned with our consumer base, and our core consumer was a mom. They wanted to support those moms with families, our main shoppers. In addition, of course, the evidence on the health side had become stark: Cigarettes were bad for your health.

Yet there were a lot of other—and in this case, important—factors to consider. Target was a business. So yes, they considered the health implications and the set of consumers Target was trying to attract, but they also had to balance those concerns with other key bottom-line factors: the costs of carrying cigarettes versus the potential sales lost. The brand, customer experience, and bottom line all came into play. They needed to critically listen and balance these various factors in the bigger picture.

The executive committee looked at the impact on the consumer of both carrying cigarettes and dropping them. They balanced the potential lost sales with the costs of ID'ing minors who weren't legally allowed to purchase cigarettes. The regulatory issues of checking ID and the differences by state were becoming complex—and expensive to adhere to. Cigarettes were also a high-theft item. There was also a general sense that taking a leadership position on the tobacco issue would be good for the brand and aligned with our core consumer. Dropping cigarettes would differentiate Target from Kmart and Walmart. Which was key as Target was planning expansion into the Northeast that year. So the leadership team made their bold choice.

Years later, when questioned, one of these leaders said they all, even the smokers, were proud of the decision. It was relatively seamless, if complex, to execute; they did a fifty-store test first. And there was probably some grumbling in locations that, like the executive committee, were full of smokers. But it was the right thing to do and made economic sense. Healthy debate had led to a sound decision. Target never looked back.

- Think about a recent discussion or debate you've had at work, with a friend, or at home with a spouse or child.

- How did you identify the problem you were trying to solve up front and get alignment on it?

- Did you take five minutes to humanize the players up front?

- Did you ask questions with genuine curiosity?

- How did you honor your truth and others' truth?

- Did you call out behaviors to call the other(s) in?

- What was difficult for you? What was easy for you? What do you need to work on?

Negotiate

A third pillar of good communication is the ability to engage in civil and productive negotiations. As with good listening and healthy debate, engagement is key. Listening to learn, empathetic listening, and critical listening will all come in handy. Good negotiators maintain their curiosity and interest in another's perspective. They also, to reach resolution, take the occasional step back to critically analyze the facts gathered against a bigger picture. And of course, the ground rules for engaging in debate outlined above also apply in negotiations.

What I find most important when negotiating is to be objective, have a point of view, and know what you're willing to give up.

My job at Target involved many, many negotiations, most of which I can't disclose. (It was a running joke with my boss that he could never do my evaluations properly because while he wanted to give me full credit for my accomplishments, he couldn't as I would never tell him exactly what I'd said or done in any specific negotiation.)

I can say, however, that one of my most interesting negotiations took place in Chicago. Chicago is a town with a tradition of tough politics and tough dealmaking. My meeting didn't take place under the most auspicious of circumstances. Target had recently closed stores that Chicago officials felt were important to their city, and they were suspicious of our future intentions. Our goal was to hear them out, to be objective. It's important not to go into it with a fixed point of view. In negotiations, you often have to challenge yourself when biased thoughts or assumptions enter your mind. But it's also important to find a way to communicate your point of view and actual intentions. Think critically about the situation at hand and know your goal.

In any negotiation, you've got to start with hearing people out. People want to be seen and heard. Letting everyone speak their piece helps you discover who's aligned and who's not—and why. Sometimes you may be working from the same set of facts, but just have a different interpretation of those facts. Sometimes you may be working from entirely different facts. For example, one person may cite a study on how a new rail line will bolster accessibility, while another party may share data about the environmental impact of the same infrastructure project. You may both have valid points, but you're coming from very different directions. Either way, you need to understand the exact nature of your differences to bridge the gap. Oftentimes in a negotiation, once the facts are made clear and inaccuracies are cast aside, the trade-offs and decisions flow more easily.

When we met with the Chicago officials there were a lot of misconceptions that had arisen in the wake of the store closings that needed to be cleared up. We needed to reassure the community that just because we were closing one store didn't mean we wouldn't be opening others in the future, or that we wouldn't find jobs in other stores for the people displaced by the closings.

The more we all discussed, the more we realized that a big part of the problem was that we were working from very different fact bases. As our team shared additional data, the other side began to lean in a bit more and trust that what we were telling them was true. Often teams do come in with very different versions of what the facts are and it can take a while to get to a shared understanding, but at least now we were in direct conversation.

Much of good negotiating is making sure that your words and actions are aligned, and that you are being transparent about where you're making progress. Like all good communication, your ability to stay objective, to listen, listen, listen, and to convey your point of view calmly and clearly builds trust and your relationship with your negotiating partner.

Using these tools, we gradually built up a working relationship with the Chicago officials. We were clear about what we were willing to give up and what we weren't. If you're not willing to budge on anything, you aren't negotiating. And the same goes if you are willing to give up everything. We didn't bridge every single difference; it's rare that any negotiation does that. But we all left the table with a willingness to move forward.

By using the rules of healthy debate, the tools of good listening, and the fundamental principles of negotiation, we were able to accomplish what at first blush looked to be the impossible.

For your next negotiation, try to:

- Be objective.
- Have a point of view.

- Get aligned on the facts.

- Be clear on what you're willing to give up and what you're not.

- Use the listening and debating tools above, such as empathetic and critical listening and humanizing the other player. Find the common ground. It's always there, no matter how tiny and hard to see.

You might surprise yourself at the positive results!

PS from Laysha

Your ability to find solutions and move forward is greatly enhanced by seeking to understand other people's stories, lived experiences, and perspectives. This has helped me connect with people in a way that minimizes polarization and discord and creates a pathway to civil discourse and resolution.

CHAPTER SEVEN

Adopt Empowering Processes

Practice isn't the thing you do once you're good.
It's the thing you do that makes you good.

—MALCOLM GLADWELL

When I first announced my retirement from Target, I was full of many emotions: gratitude, loss, optimism for the future, appreciation of the past. I knew there would be sadness in leaving. But also the excitement of what would come. Then the loveliest, most unexpected thing happened. Notes started to pour in. People I'd worked with. People I'd supported. People I'd mentored and sponsored. Some wrote me eloquent emails and others posted on my social media thanking me for my service, my dedication, my impact—and my mentorship.

Now, I'm not one to dwell on what I've given to others. There's still so much to be done. As I've said, my purpose is to be of service, and that continues, whatever the work I'm engaged in. But it did make me think about the mentorship lessons I wanted to pass on to you, the readers of this book. I think of management as being about overseeing tasks, setting expectations, and ensuring processes are followed to deliver consistent results. Leadership is about motivating and helping others grow, establishing a clear vision, and focusing on long-term goals. Because leading others is a vital part of sustaining meaningful leadership over time. And people leadership for me is akin to mentorship and sponsorship; it's about lifting others up so that they too can be their best and championing them forward to have their own impact.

Maintaining and sustaining a healthy team over long periods of time and the inevitable changes you'll face, however, requires that the individuals in your team feel empowered to do their best work. One way to confirm this is happening is to examine your processes to ensure you are using best practices. Let me explain.

Routines and processes can be empowering. They can simplify and streamline communication, offer support and alignment, and free people up to focus on their work. Frameworks liberate the members of your team to do what needs to be done. Regular routines, accountability check-ins, and a continuing focus on goals and objectives introduce clarity and predictability. Well-designed frameworks and processes also open up true partnerships between team members and their team leader. When the framework is clear and mutually understood, everyone is working toward the same end.

Let's take a closer look at some best practices for routines and processes that have sustained me throughout my career. Though some may be familiar, you may be surprised at how many you may have glossed over or missed out on in the contemporary rush to stay afloat.

Have an Agenda

Even the simplest routines can help you and your team run smoothly. Have an agenda for every meeting you hold. Whether you're in a small organization or a large one, asking for and thinking through an agenda will help you accomplish more. Following an agenda gets everyone on the same page—and keeps things moving as you explore priorities, assign tasks, and clarify assignments. I even use agendas in my one-on-one meetings with my direct reports. To create a very simple agenda, ask yourself this series of questions:

- What's the goal for today? (Are you giving an update, seeking input or needing a decision?)
- How are we going to get it done?
- Who's going to do what?
- What's the priority?

If you've ever been stuck in an agendaless meeting or phone call, you know exactly how frustrating it can be as the clock ticks down and nothing is accomplished. Instead, before you get on that Zoom, be clear about what you want to accomplish. And how much time you have to accomplish it in, whether that's thirty minutes or an hour.

Also note that creating an agenda might help you decide whether you need a meeting at all. *Don't have meetings for the sake of having meetings.* If your agenda turns into an email that you can just send or a phone call that you can make, take the win.

Consider sending a quick email before the Zoom asking others what they want to discuss. Then send out the agenda several days (or more) in advance, depending on the subject matter, to ensure that participants have adequate time to prep. Decide whether you need a notetaker during the meeting, and if so select that person before the meeting starts.

At the end of the meeting, establish the expectation that the notetaker will share a recap with attendees. What decisions were supposed to have been made? Were they? And if not, now what? Don't forget about follow-up research that may be required and making sure someone has been assigned to that. Outline your next steps. And associate timelines with those, if appropriate. All this will help you solve the problem or convey the opportunity you held the meeting to address. A process for follow-up helps keep your actions on track.

Software programs can help track your projects, assignments, and tasks. Know, however, that you do not necessarily need complicated software. You just need the will, the organizational skills, clear processes, and probably email (!) to keep others and yourself accountable as you set agendas and keep the work moving forward.

> • For your next meeting, whether it's Zoom or otherwise, prepare an agenda, send it out in advance, assign a no-taker, then at the end of the meeting do a recap and outline the follow-up.
>
> • Check back in a week. Did you accomplish your goals? If so, bravo! If not, why not?

Set and Align Work and Life Goals

As a team leader, you always want to clearly communicate and mutually establish goals and objectives for your team members that are in alignment with the company's strategic priorities. A team member's performance is measured on these goals and objectives, so you want there to be clarity, and ideally for them to be fully engaged in establishing them. If you're part of an organization, be sure you understand the preferred methodology and approach for annual goal-setting.

I also talk with every team member and mentee about setting and aligning their work and life goals. Together we create an individual goals and development plan. This document includes their goals and objectives as aligned with company priorities and strategies, but also their larger, long-term life and career goals.

An individual goals and development plan is a road map for team members—and for leaders—for their life and career journey. I always encourage people to think not just about what they want from their job, but what they want out of life. This plan should capture that vision. Goals should capitalize on an individual's strengths and address their development needs. If you're a team leader, encourage your team members to build a plan that goes beyond their annual performance goals; if you're a team member and your team leader hasn't suggested this, you can create it for yourself and discuss it with your leader.

There is no one right way to create an individual goals and development plan or life and career road map. But these steps have been useful to me in my own journey, and in guiding others:

Identify annual work and life goals. A goals and development plan should include high-level objectives and actions for the year, with clearly defined metrics and a check-in frequency to stay accountable. Include both job-specific and life goals. Don't forget to include well-being goals as part of the priorities.

Identify the key relationships needed to accomplish those goals. If you are guiding someone else's plan, I recommend making suggestions for contacts that will help them meet their goals or even put them in touch with relevant players. For example, perhaps there are other sponsors who could be involved in some of their key goals. Come up with a plan for how often the sponsor, including yourself as team leader, should be updated on the team member's progress. What about peer mentors and others who can provide helpful counsel through the year?

Plan for long-term career goals. Talk through the strategies or actions the team member might need to take now to be ready for the role or career they want in the future. Not just titles, but what career experiences and impact do they want to have? How will they develop the skills that will prepare them to deliver the impact they ultimately want to make while staying aligned with the organization's objectives?

Make note of any learning opportunities to develop new skills. Encourage your team member to participate in key training sessions or read books that will help them build new knowledge or skills. If you are doing your own plan, research this for yourself and hold yourself accountable to the learning you want for yourself. Be specific about which trainings and which books and set deadlines.

Track progress and evolve the goals on a regular basis. Review the plan quarterly or at whatever frequency makes sense for both you and the team member. Are they on track? How can they get on track, if not? Are they adequately challenged and are their goals still in alignment with corporate goals? Organizations change and people change, so regular check-ins are the best way to keep moving forward on both work and life priorities. As life's situations arise, plans can and should be adapted.

Continuous conversations on goals and objectives should be a priority for all involved. These ongoing conversations are how you empower people and help them grow. They are also how you stay in alignment with the company's priorities.

In the beginning of my career, when I was a community relations manager in Chicago, working on Marshall Field's philanthropic and community investment strategy, I hired a graduate student from the Art Institute of Chicago named Angelique Williams, now Angelique Power. Angelique worked part time for us. She was your typical art student, a self-described "tourist in corporate culture." She had wonderful, untamed hair, cat-eye glasses, and would often take her shoes off at work. Because her clothes were better suited to an artist's studio than a corporate office, I loaned her some of my own. She was also deeply intelligent, thoughtful, ambitious, creative, and, like me, invested in our authenticity as Black women, as corporate pioneers, and in doing well by doing good.

Angelique was also on a journey. And that journey involved an ever-changing goals and development plan, and an awareness of what the company's goals and objectives were so that we were continually staying aligned.

Angelique wasn't totally sure yet what her career would look like (who is at that age?), but she knew it would involve art in some fashion. Working at Marshall Field's was a job she'd initially picked up to supplement her income as she attended school. But she was soon absorbing all our routines and processes around grant-making, learning how things in a company get done, just as I'd done before her. She took classes to learn more about social impact work.

As Angelique acquired all the skills and abilities we'd outlined and more, she found herself and her life's work in a career that lies in a space between art and the grantor role. She has since been in numerous impressive roles: She's led communications and community engagement at the Museum of Contemporary Art Chicago, been a program director at the Joyce Foundation, and president of the Chicago-based Field Foundation. Currently CEO at the Skillman Foundation in Detroit, she has combined her art and business background to great effect, understanding both sides of the grantor/grantee equation.

We remain close. And though today she buys her own clothes and wears shoes, I occasionally continue to provide guidance for her and feel all the delight in seeing her shine and find her clear path forward. And I am the beneficiary of her wisdom and lived experience as well. As people managers we are also ideally mentors and sponsors, and the gift of having mentored well is one that continually gives back with each and every one of the mentees and individuals you've sponsored.

Once you and your team member are aligned on company goals and objectives, use the five steps to create an individual goals and development plan. If you are a team member and your team leader isn't doing this with you, talk to them about doing it jointly or do one on your own and, if possible, share it with them and make them a partner in your growth.

1. Identify annual life and work goals.

2. Identify the key relationships needed to accomplish those goals.

3. Plan for long-term career goals.

4. Make note of any learning opportunities to develop new skills.

5. Track progress and evolve the goals on a regular basis.

Clear Processes *Enable* Partnerships

When Angelique first came on board, I asked her to help me review the many grant applications that were submitted to Marshall Field's for our local community programs. I knew as an art student she'd get the creative piece of what we were doing. Though Angelique had never seen the process from the side of the grantor before, she was a quick study. Because she had no business background, however, we had many conversations on our goals and objectives for the grant review process so that she could understand what I was looking for and be on the same page with the rest of our small staff, as she developed her own skill set accordingly. Together we were all developing a clear and data-driven but also grounded evaluation process that allowed us to be consistent in our evaluations and enable partnerships with our grantees.

Today a lot of grant applications utilize what we call a "common application" process, allowing a single form that can be used by many grant makers. The common applications are effective, as many grant makers' routines and processes have over time themselves streamlined and merged. But back in our Marshall Field's days, the applications to each grant maker were much more varied. So our tiny office, which consisted of Kassie, me, Kassie's assistant, and now Angelique part time, had to create our own processes and frameworks for ensuring that our grant reviews were fair and objective. We ourselves were small and scrappy and wearing five hundred hats. But I wanted to make sure that we were being professional, thoughtful, and thorough in considering every application that came our way.

To ensure that everyone was aligned on Marshall Field's goals and objectives for the grants we received, I would talk to Angelique about making sure that we were moving beyond theory to practical application. As part of our grant-reviewing process, we were, whenever possible, having a conversation with the applicant organization, or doing a site visit, or even chatting with their partners or the community being served by the grant. Making that kind of direct contact and observation was an important part of our routine. It helped us move from theory to practical application. We weren't just judging an organization based on what we read on a piece of paper. We were seeing exactly how the applicant had brought their ideas and passions to life. We made it a point to meet with people in the community rather than at our office. By meeting them in their space, we could see the reality of what they were doing and had done. Angelique knew how to assess the theoretical side, but I wanted to make sure she was developing the community-facing side as well, and indeed she took to it wonderfully.

I would also push Angelique to look at the applicants' business basics. What were the nonprofit organization's financials? And I don't mean just checking off what they said on their application. I wanted her to investigate the figures we were being given. Was the applicant in the red? Or in the black? Meaning, were they in debt? Or were they covering their expenses with their grants and income? We also needed to know where they were getting their money from. How much as a percentage of their total spend was coming from corporations versus foundations versus the government? Was there an appropriate mix in their portfolio?

Alignment with Marshall Field's community relations goals, as always, was key. We needed to ensure that we weren't just looking at the mission or the purpose of the organization but also how they were articulating their goals and objectives. We wanted to know that the applicant's goals and objectives were aligned with ours, much as I talked to Angelique about aligning her goals and objectives with the company's.

For example, Marshall Field's was interested in improving educational outcomes, and curriculum integration through the arts was something we were supporting at the time. Supporting art and culture was a good thing in and of itself, of course. However, an arts program might also have an application to a course in another subject and, through curriculum integration, be used to teach history or math or whatever the relevant subject might be. For example, if a theater program had developed an application that dramatized history, the result might be that the attending students would develop a deeper understanding of both theater and social studies.

From our perspective, we'd want to see how that arts organization was articulating and showing how many students they were serving and how they were helping the subject teachers. And if they were proposing a history lesson come to life, how were they going to measure their progress or success with the students' understanding of the historical figures and event? Through our discussions of goals and objectives, I was encouraging Angelique to look at what was written, but also to apply critical thinking to the proposals.

Digging deep and applying critical thinking was also why I wanted her to get out and meet with the organizations wherever possible or get on the phone with them. I liken the process to digging beneath standardized test scores. Some people are great test takers, and they do an awesome job on tests where it's multiple choice or an essay format. But others simply aren't great test takers. And they don't do well on written essays. But if they could have talked you through their plans, they might have done very well. People learn in different ways and perform in different ways. We wanted to create an application space that would get the best out of all kinds of entrepreneurial folks, even if they didn't have a grant writer, which some organizations don't.

Sometimes I'd be completely wowed by a grant application. It was beautifully written, the grammar was on point, and their theory of change was effectively articulated. But if you dug deeper, the work and the results didn't measure up. On the other hand, we often found that someone would come across as average on paper, but then when we looked at the work, we'd realize it—and its impact—was phenomenal and something we absolutely wanted to support. You just needed to get beneath what was being submitted on paper.

Angelique had the capacity to do all this. She simply hadn't been in this space before and hadn't been asked to think about these reviews in this specific way. Her story is a great reminder that when you're onboarding someone, you can't assume that they have had the opportunity or the expertise to do a role, especially if you're hiring them as someone with potential. Angelique came in ready to learn and contribute. I assured her we could talk about whatever questions she had as she acquired these skills so that she felt comfortable with the evaluative framework. I also wanted her to understand that I too relished our conversations and debates over criteria. Just because I'd been evaluating grants longer than she had, it didn't mean that she might not have a different perspective or way of thinking about it that could make the work better, or have us even thinking about the reviews in a different way.

Our accountability through this back-and-forth became a shared accountability. We became true partners in the process, even as I was her team leader. As I've said, ideally your processes and frameworks don't entrap your team members; they empower them.

The same was true of our grantees. As the grantor, we were often in a perceived place of power. We were doing the review. We were making the decision. But we were also their partners. We wanted them to meet their goals and objectives. Particularly if they had been granted the year prior, we were always working with them to ensure that they had established realistic metrics and were meeting them. Again, it was all about articulating a clear vision, and then setting realistic goals and objectives so that everyone was aligned and partnering on a clear path forward, even as they worked on their individual development. The evaluation process we developed enabled many partnerships that delivered meaningful impact, whether at the individual program level or through systemic change.

Growth Requires Data, but Remember, Progress over Perfection

When you work with a team member or mentee to set and reestablish goals and objectives, you are often looking for progress over perfection. This can be especially important when mentoring anyone in the early stages of their business or career, though it's true at any stage. Everyone has setbacks and faces obstacles. It's your objective as a team leader to help your team members through their obstacles and keep them moving forward toward the goal.

Two of my mentees are a terrific illustration of how hard work and keeping an eye on both the hard data and progress over perfection pay off. I first got connected to Alejandro Vélez and Nikhil Arora in 2015 through Antonio Tijerino, president and CEO of the Hispanic Heritage Foundation, and Kate Heiny, Target's sustainability director. Alejo and Nik had just graduated from UC Berkeley's Haas undergraduate business school. Antonio thought we'd be a good match and he trusted me to help them and offer sound advice about best practices in business. Tony is a creative and resourceful leader, collaborator, and ally. Under Tony's leadership, the Hispanic Heritage Foundation has created pathways of opportunity and lifted up the contributions and stories of Latinos for decades.

Alejo and Nik were bright, full of ambition, and eager to see their new venture, Back to the Roots, a gardening supply company, succeed. They were just a few years out from starting their business out of UC Berkeley (as an urban mushroom farm of all things!), and Back to the Roots, with a focus on organic soil, organic seeds, and nurturing urban gardeners, had just launched their first product at Target. Their vision was to take their brand national and partner with many major retailers. But they had some spadework to do first.

Initially, we spent a lot of time discussing their goals and objectives, and routines around those goals and objectives. Of key importance was that they get used to looking at the data and really understanding what was happening in their business and what was possible through data analytics. Last year's sales of a specific product might be a baseline. But then I was continually asking them questions I would ask no matter what company you're in: As a total business, and by a particular category, what is your goal against last year's? And what's your goal in the marketplace?

Even when I first met Alejo and Nik, I thought they could expand. They were young and green, but also so smart and driven. And they were passionate about growing what they were doing and creating more urban gardeners. As we discussed in chapter 1, you need to take a bet on yourself; similarly, as a leader you learn to take bets on other people. Sometimes that means going with your gut because you just know that people have that potential. I know that when I see that scrappiness and entrepreneurial need and passion in others like I saw in Alejo and Nik, I go with that feeling and invest. These guys were total entrepreneurs—and they were working on a business that would serve inner-city folks looking for fresh food and greenery, a great purpose and mission.

Alejo and Nik did have a business background from their undergraduate studies. They also learned quickly. What they needed was infrastructure and a better understanding of how to build that infrastructure.

When one of their first products landed at Whole Foods, it was a major get. But keeping it there and scaling the business is a whole other story. My questions to Alejo and Nik and my emphasis on data analytics involved a lot of tough love. I was always pushing them to define and be as specific as possible about their goals and objectives. How were they going to scale the business? I would advise them to look at what they were saying they were doing, but then examine through data if they were accomplishing what they'd outlined. How did they plan to stay in Whole Foods if that was an objective? What other national businesses did they want entry into, whether a Target, Walmart, Home Depot, Lowe's, Costco, and so on, and how could they build in that direction? Did they have a distribution model and manufacturers that were working well for them? And could they distribute and manufacture at scale? I wanted them to look at the data analytics around their business and examine how those insights aligned with who they perceived to be their core consumer. They also needed to look at how their business category aligned with the business categories of the firms and organizations they wanted to enter and at what scale. Because whoever your buyer is, they've also got a goal of what they are trying to accomplish in a total category, and you need to know what percent of that total category you are. Perhaps a partnership was a possibility, and if so, could they scale at the demand the partner would require and meet not only the size of the buy but the quality, because there would be quality controls? Would they be able to meet the delivery timetables?

There's so much involved in growth other than just saying, "I want to get bigger." And it all needs to be quantified. What you want to grow, how you are going to grow it, and what it takes to do that are all questions you need answers to. And again, it all comes back to goals, objectives, and tough love around the data analytics. It also comes back to recognizing that your goal is to make progress, not achieve perfection. Growth of this kind never comes without setbacks and obstacles. And Alejo and Nik, like all entrepreneurs, faced challenges with scaling, quality control, meeting delivery timetables, and more as they pushed forward with their growth plan.

I recently emailed with Alejo and Nik, just to check in on how they were doing and to see if our memories of the early mentorship period aligned. I was struck not only by the similarity of our recollections—they too mentioned all the tough love I gave them around data!—but also by the fact that they mentioned that I bolstered their confidence. That I helped reinforce for them that they mattered and that their mission mattered. And that that guidance helped them walk into any meeting feeling like they belonged, even when, as first-time founders and entrepreneurs, it was an ultra-intimidating meeting with people whose merchandising decisions were made for two thousand stores nationally.

A lot of confidence comes from having relationships that bolster you, and as a leader cheerleading is part of the job. But it also comes down to letting mentees know that it can't all happen at once, and there is no route that is obstacle-free. The goal is to keep everyone's eyes on progress, not perfection. If you can keep the focus on balancing short- and long-term goals and objectives, you'll find success.

Back to the Roots is now the largest and fastest-growing 100 percent organic garden company in the United States, with notable board members such as Sol Trujillo and Ayesha Curry, and investors such as J Balvin and Gabrielle Union! I couldn't be prouder of Alejo and Nik and their growth over the nearly ten years I've known them. They are doing well by doing good.

Define Roles and Responsibilities

I sometimes hear leaders talking about how an employee hasn't taken responsibility for a task. My first question back is whether that task was clearly assigned and/or part of the team member's goals and objectives. When someone isn't taking responsibility, it's sometimes part and parcel of a larger communication issue: that is, they don't know they were responsible for that task in the first place! A team member's goals and objectives need to be clearly set and communicated if they and their team leader are to stay aligned.

You may have heard of a process called RASCI. It stands for Responsible, Accountable, Supportive, Consulted, and Informed. RASCI is one of many frameworks for assigning the roles and responsibilities of the various stakeholders in a project or task. There are others, but this is the one I use. It helps you define who's working on what. Whoever is Responsible is the project owner. This is ideally one person but can be more. They are the manager of others' work on the task or the one performing it. The Accountable person has final control over a project task—and the resources associated with it. They are usually the person who is delegating the project work; ideally this is just one person. The buck stops with the Accountable. The Accountable person and Responsible person are not the same; they check and balance each other. Supportive people assist the Responsible in completing a specific project or provide resources to them. Their goals are aligned with the Responsible. The Consulted help the

Responsible successfully finish tasks, often by bringing their project expertise to bear. They are consulted at the earliest stages. Finally, there are the Informed, who need to be kept in the loop about a project at all stages, up to and including completion. The Informed are key stakeholders and/or people who will be impacted by a project's successful completion.

RASCI helps you clearly define roles and responsibilities for any project. It clarifies who's working on what, eliminates any confusion or overlap, and can even reduce conflict. It can also help set priorities for the individuals involved. If I'm Responsible or Supportive, I know I need to prioritize the project deadlines. There's even an opportunity to lift people up with RASCI. You can make a more junior person the Accountable for a project and see how they do.

Clearly charting roles can also help you identify any individual who might be getting overburdened with task assignments. Such identification can be a project-saver. Sometimes team members, especially those who are eager to please, are reluctant to tell you they simply have too much already on their plate to take on additional tasks for which they are designated the Responsible one. These shy-to-speak-up folks may mean well, but then when the inevitable due date comes and expectations aren't met, all hell can break loose. If you are a team member who's being overburdened, you will serve yourself and others best if you voice your concerns up front. It doesn't help the team if you wait until it's too late and important tasks you've been assigned are simply falling by the wayside. If you are team leader, having a clear matrix of expectations for your various team members can avoid this kind of overburdening.

I use RASCI all the time. It was the routine and process that guided all our big projects at Target, including cross-organizational ones. It was used so frequently that it became a common tool and language across departments within the organization. We embraced it because it allowed us to communicate clearly and provided plenty of what I call "alignment moments." It created a system and a discipline so that we all had absolute clarity on project responsibilities and roles. It also took out some of the complexity from an already complex organization, adding in simplicity instead.

- Use the RASCI process for your next big project at work or even for a community event.

- Assign the Responsible, Accountable, Supportive, Consulted, and Informed individuals. What did you learn?

- Did things go more smoothly due to the increased clarity of roles? What would you change if you used RASCI again?

Connect the Dots

Especially as your company or organization grows, leaders need to connect the dots for the team members who aren't part of the leadership team. A team member's goals and objectives must connect to company strategy. It doesn't work if the company overall has determined its growth lies in one direction, but an employee is independently working to grow in another, not realizing they aren't aligned. A good friend of mine is a business consultant and she's described situations where the leadership of a small company will plot a new growth plan and then forget or fail to inform its employees. Another company she works with had instituted leadership meetings, but a lot of their employees were spread out and working from home and the leadership had no mechanism for sharing leadership decisions and other key information (remember the "now what" question in our discussion of meeting follow-up above!). How are the employees to know they need to adjust and realign unless the leaders connect the dots for them?

Informing those who work for and with you of a strategic change in direction can also open opportunities for them to shine. For example, when Target discussed moving into fresh food, I held a meeting with my team. What would this do to our philanthropic strategy? What would the direct impact be? The more we discussed it, the more excited we got. It would impact our hunger strategy and food donations, and in a positive way. Opportunities would open for us, including new partnerships and expansion of old ones. Once the dots were connected and the changes in strategy communicated, we could get to work realigning our goals and objectives—ultimately to great success. Target now donates millions of pounds of food each year, providing millions of meals to families in need through a partnership with Feeding America.

- Take an overall look at your routines and processes. Are there communication gaps that need to be filled?

- Are there decisions that one department or group is making that others need to be informed about?

- How as team leader can you establish communication mechanisms that connect the dots for your team members and better ensure that everyone is on the same page and taking advantage of the organization's new direction and growth?

Routines and processes empower. Frameworks enable freedom. Setting down our goals and objectives and having data-anchored plans for expansion helps us grow. The trick is developing and using those processes in a way that ensures that you too are sustainably empowering your team members—and leading with meaning.

PS from Laysha

While I talk about and believe in empowering others, it's also important to remember that your team has a role to play in their own empowerment too. As leaders, we provide the guardrails, the tools, and the encouragement—but our teams have to walk through the door, using the developed practices and processes, and take the initiative to drive results. That's what empowerment is all about.

PART FOUR

SUSTAIN YOURSELF AND OTHERS

CHAPTER EIGHT

Nurture The Culture

*The ability of a group of people to do
remarkable things hinges on how well those
people can pull together as a team.*

—SIMON SINEK

My dad was a firefighter for over thirty-five years. As a result, I grew up in and around firehouses and first responders. I even have my dad's lieutenant firefighter helmet hanging up in my house as a constant reminder of his bravery and service. Firefighters work twenty-four-hour shifts. They eat, sleep, socialize, train, and work at the firehouse, then spend time in the community fighting fires, doing fire safety, and more. All of which results in a unique culture. You have to really know and trust your colleagues when you're literally doing life-and-death work. The firefighting culture is developed out of a shared purpose, relationships, and the sustaining and championing of others' impact. It's a culture that fosters leading with meaning.

Culture is the collective set of behaviors of an organization; it's also their common set of beliefs, values, or norms. Carolyn Dewar and Reed Doucette of McKinsey describe culture, in part, as the iceberg mass both above and below the surface of a company's waters. Culture includes the observable beliefs and behaviors of a team, "the *what* and *how* above the surface," as well as that which cannot be seen. The "unseen shared beliefs and mindsets" are just as important an influence on an organization's culture as what you can observe. Unlike the captain of the *Titanic*, you want to be aware of and influencing that iceberg mass below if you're trying to navigate those waters and steer everyone safely to shore.

Culture isn't something that can be taken for granted; it needs to be shaped, nurtured, and mutually built. And everyone plays a role, at every level, whether you're trying to articulate your culture, shift it in a meaningful way, or do your part to make it better.

A strong culture simultaneously contributes to the organization's growth and its team members' personal and professional growth and fulfillment. It fosters team engagement, allows organizations to recruit and retain top talent, and drives financial performance.

Developing a strong, unique, and shared culture is a primary leadership goal; cultures allow you to bring the organization's purpose, values, and strategy to life. When you're leading with meaning, you're bringing humanity and integrity to your everyday actions and thus bringing that to your organization whether you're leading from above or below.

There's a lot to be learned from the firefighter culture I grew up with. Obviously, I'm not advocating for twenty-four-hour shifts for everyone, but their culture has much to teach us about how, as a leader looking to lead with meaning, one can manage and nurture a healthy team.

One point of clarification, up front: When I refer to your team, I don't just mean your direct reports or the people who work for you, though as I've mentioned, Target has always referred to their employees as team members. Rather, your team consists of the much larger circle of people you influence. Nurturing the culture means nurturing the connections you've forged both inside and outside your company or organization. If you're only thinking about your direct reports when it comes to leading with meaning, you're missing a huge opportunity to lead and serve. Much of what you might need to influence and many of the people you will be talking to lie outside the inner circle of people who work directly for you. When I say team, I encourage you to think in the widest terms possible. Your team is anyone you might influence in your everyday life.

Let's begin with how to develop a healthy team culture and the three values that many meaning-driven cultures nurture and share: caring, learning, and trust.

A Culture of Care+

Caring is where it all starts. I often think back to my dad's firefighter family. What an extraordinary part of the firefighter culture the firefighter family is! The people who worked with my dad not only got to know each other, they also got to know each other's families. Many firefighters work two or three jobs—and stay firefighters for decades. So everyone grows up together. Including the firefighter families, who all take care of each other. They are at each other's kids' graduations, school performances, and sporting events. They come to the kids' basketball games and root for them. If somebody is sick, everyone comes and checks in, doing what they can to support the ill person. The firefighter family is extended family.

And with firefighters, it's care for life. Recently, when a firefighter advocate heard my dad passed, he immediately reached out to my mom, me, and my siblings, asking, "What do you guys need? How can we support you? Whatever you need, we're here to help. Based on the benefits that are in your father's name, here's all the information you and your mom are gonna to need to know. And here are the phone numbers you'll want. Do you want us to come to your house and go through this with you? When should we come?"

We ended up meeting at the firehouse and they gave us a whole list of things they would do. They told us it would be their honor to come to the wake and the service. And wow did they show up. Thirty firemen, in full uniform, lined the funeral home and took fifteen-minute shifts on each side of my father's casket, guarding it. Then all of them came in together to pay their tributes to us and our family.

I was floored. Sure, my dad had served for thirty-five years, but he had also been retired for probably twenty years after that. Yet in firefighter culture, that time lapse didn't exist. The care continued. It's astounding.

Even the food we served at my dad's wake is a firefighter-care story. I knew about a BBQ joint called Firehouse BBQ & Blues that was owned by an ex-firefighter, and I fell in love with the idea of having food from his place. What could be more appropriate? Only problem was, it was the holidays, and there were parties and all the usual holiday madness at the restaurant. It was a long shot. But I was determined to try. I knew my dad would have appreciated the firefighter connection. We gave them a call, and of course their first response was, "No capacity, we're fully booked."

Then the woman on the phone softened. "What is this for?" she asked.

I told her.

"Oh, it's for someone who passed? What's his name?"

"Eugene. He's a retired fireman," I said.

"Oh, we know Eugene. He was at Firehouse One! Give me a second," she replied. She hung up and called back in less than thirty minutes.

"Of course we'll do it!" she said. "We will make this happen."

After the service, Firehouse One had us come to the station house. They have a memorial wall there where they honor and recognize their past family members. They wanted to show us where my dad's name was. Visiting the wall was emotional, as was walking the halls of the second firehouse I'd grown up in (the first was Firehouse Four) for what felt like the last time. We were all incredibly touched.

I'm still floored at the love and respect our firefighter family showed us. It's an extraordinary culture of care.

Equaling the care of a firefighter family is a difficult task. Yet caring for, supporting, and trying to understand others, as the firefighter example shows, is essential to leading with meaning. I call this care+.

Care+ is about understanding and respecting the whole person and their whole life—and the group. It goes back to the fact that everyone has their own calling and their own purpose, and yet as we work toward common goals, we are aligned. The ideal workplace culture respects the individuality of each player even as it creates the conditions that motivate everyone to play on the same team.

At Target, one of our key mantras, developed under the leadership of CEO Brian Cornell, was "Care, Grow, and Win Together." We took it seriously and built one of the most effective retail cultures among our competitors. Culture sustains your team and is how you begin to champion them.

It's easier be a carrier of culture when times are good and business is strong than when times are tough. I speak from experience, having lived through crucible moments such as Hurricane Katrina, 9/11, the

Great Recession, proxy battles, a data breach, the pandemic, and sociopolitical challenges and shifts. When you have a strong culture, opportunity can come out of crisis moments like these. But if you haven't done the work to build and sustain an effective culture, these monumental events can paralyze an organization.

It may sound strange to hear that culture is built. Let me reassure you: It is. Or at least actively guided. One interesting thing about culture is that it will exist whether you tend to it or not. Culture is just the way things get done. And things will get done with guidance or without. So it's preferable if there's guidance on how and why certain things are done. You always want to be actively influencing a team's beliefs. If you're nurturing your team and the culture in a direction that fits the organizational purpose, values, and goals, you're going to be more effective in staying true to them.

When you actively guide values from the top, it influences how people respond to the culture. And that response matters. Because culture isn't something that can simply be dictated from above. As I like to say, it can be "on the walls, but that doesn't mean it's alive in the halls." It's got to be something felt across the entire team. The caring needs to permeate your organization. People and their behaviors *are* the culture and the care needs to come from below as much as it does from the top, much as it did with the firefighters.

How does a culture of care+ become mutual? It starts with a coherent vision, so that everyone understands the shared overall goal, the accompanying cultural values, and their own specific role in achieving that vision. It also requires empowerment. The more you take the time to listen to your team and recognize their efforts on behalf of the shared goal, the more you empower them. And the more empowered they feel, the more that culture of care+ will be alive in the halls.

And by the way, you can contribute to this culture of care+ even if you're not in charge. Your actions and decisions contribute to how culture comes to life on a day-to-day basis. And, again, you may have opportunities to introduce values and beliefs associated with leading with meaning through your actions.

When you lead with care+ and empower others, it becomes a self-sustaining set of beliefs and attitudes. I know because I've lived it.

I still remember, back in the day, when I was first part of the Marshall Field's store team in Chicago. It was June 1991, after the Dayton-Hudson Corporation had acquired Marshall Field's but before Dayton-Hudson had rebranded as Target Corporation. I worked at the Water Tower Place store on Michigan Avenue, in an elegant seventy-four-story skyscraper with a glass elevator that made you feel like you were ascending into the sky—our store alone was eight stories tall. The outer atrium had marble floors and walls and chandeliers. Upon entering, shoppers felt enveloped in the height of luxury and treated to a joyous getaway from their otherwise hectic and pressure-filled day.

The first department I was in was called Women's Better Sportswear. So, in addition to being part of the whole store team, I was in the subsidiary team of the Women's Better Sportswear area. I was in a sales leader role; the equivalent today would be something like an assistant department manager. And because the store was where we worked, the store was our office. When we had a team meeting, it took place on the sales floor.

We did have an office in the back. It was a narrow space with our extra product strewn around and merchandise stacked in the corner—sort of a storage room meets office with a couple of chairs and a little itty-bitty bare barely-a-desk that seemed like a leftover from an elementary school. There were even a few rodents from time to time. There were spreadsheets and sales reports of all the categories of the business taped up on the wall or pinned to a corkboard, a habit I continue to this day with sticky notes. If we had to go over a report or have a private meeting, we'd retreat to that tiny little hole-in-the-wall for a hopefully quick discussion. But our general meetings all took place on the selling floor, amidst the stylish Better Sportswear, the festive displays, and, during the holiday season, perhaps even a white-frosted Christmas tree with red bows.

Every morning would start with a team huddle. These are check-ins with the team, with everyone on the floor, akin to a restaurant's predinner meeting where servers and staff go over the details of the day's staffing and the list of specials. John C. was my store manager then. We'd gather around. We'd talk about purpose and our shared goals. John would recognize the special achievements of individuals and celebrate the wins of the team. Then he'd share any exciting news from the company, including special sales (Target now calls them LTOs, or Limited Time Offers), or launches from desirable designers, or whatever was new over the holidays. We'd find out who was out for the day due to illness or what part of the floor needed coverage. The meetings were never long, but they added to the sense of community. We were in this together. And though many on the floor worked on a commission, it wasn't just a competition, it was a collaboration as well. By the end of the huddle, as a team, we felt both cared for and empowered. We'd finish feeling stoked to go out and care for our guests.

Because the store was the office, our team wasn't just our employees, it was the entire ecosystem. We'd walk the store so that we could see the connectedness between what we did and what the rest of the store was doing.

The guest was our muse. We'd interact with the guests in our own department, of course. But we'd also chat with the guests who were checking out the store on all the levels, some who were coming in to grab a bite on their lunch hour, and some who were coming in to stroll through the perfume sprayers. The culture in the Water Tower Place store where I worked had a fast, fun, and friendly feeling.

Coincidentally, several years later, "Fast, Fun & Friendly" became the official Target mantra. Yet for me personally, it was in Water Tower Place—way before "Fast, Fun & Friendly" was Target's motto (or what would now be called a culture statement)—that I absorbed those values. My job truly was *fun*. I was the problem-solver for the businessperson or traveler who needed a new shirt because they'd just gotten an ink stain on the one that matched their new suit right before an important meeting or first job interview. Together, we'd track down an exact match. Then I'd send the new shirt off to be steamed and pressed for them in-house. A quick change later, they'd be on their way, with me wishing them good luck on their big occasion.

Or you'd have the guest who'd come in to get a small break or do a bit of window shopping. And together you'd conspire with them to discover the perfect item they sought, or maybe hadn't thought of yet. The perfect birthday gift that also perfectly fit their limited budget. Or the special gift or memento for an anniversary or special moment in someone's life. I remember one night when, after Better Sportswear, I was working upstairs in Intimate Apparel and Petites. Oprah lived in a condo in Water Tower Place and she'd often pop in to the store for something special later at night. That thrilling evening, I was able to sell her apparel. And nope, I never divulged her, nor any customer's, size or color. But it sure was fun. That claim to fame has lasted a good long while!

Of course, it also had to be *fast*. Our guests were on the clock, whether it was their lunch break or just a quick trip before or after their shift, and so were we. Fast didn't mean transactional. I never thought of our interactions that way. It meant ensuring the guest was getting what they needed promptly and that they had our full attention. As we say nowadays, we were fully present for our guests. Our goal was always to help them get what they needed in their limited time frame.

Finally, it was *friendly*. You'd say, "Hello! How are you?" as you'd meet people going up the escalator, down the escalator, or simply walking by. "How's your experience?" You'd walk and talk with them. And all the time we were learning: learning about our guests and their preferences. And because these values were something we all deeply felt, and wanted our guests to feel, the culture wasn't just a creation from the top down, it was bottom up. It was our lived experience.

Again, this was my personal experience at the Water Tower Place store. In 1994, "Fast, Fun & Friendly" under CEO Bob Ulrich became Target's official actionable, sticky, and memorable culture statement. By then, it was a way of framing a culture that represented the heart and soul of the company. It was a barometer of behavior and was reinforced from the top. Management expected us to have fast, fun, friendly attitudes, and supported all efforts to that end. There were in-store recognition moments and cards and certificates where people could be recognized for being fast, fun, and friendly, which all made a difference. As I've said, culture needs to be guided.

But you can't create these things from the top down alone. Culture is what allows you to bring your purpose and values and strategy together. And it has to be created in a way that truly resonates with the team. Or it simply won't work.

Later on, after I'd become a director in 1999, I'd go to stores with the express purpose of checking out their fast, fun, and friendly cul-

ture. I could tell right from the start whether any specific store was—
or wasn't. A lot depended on the leader. If the managers were engaging
and empowering their teams, you'd go into a store and you'd immediately feel this high energy. People would look you in the eye, and
they were happy to tell you about their area.

"Hello! Here's what I'm working on, and here's what guests are
loving," they'd say, unprompted.

The team in those stores were eager to share the details of their
day and experiences. And that's how you knew fast, fun, and friendly
had sunk deep below the surface, into the unfathomable but crucial
depths of the iceberg of that store, and permeated its behaviors and
attitudes. The team in those stores had absorbed deep in their mar-
row how to welcome people, how to make people feel comfortable in
this space, and how to get to know people. The teams in those stores
were cared for and cared.

Again, culture needs to resonate with the entire team. Yet to do so,
it needs to be guided. If you are higher up in the management food
chain this may mean that you are championing and empowering not
only your team members but also your team leaders. It's crucial that
everyone feels like their leadership matters. Everyone does matter.
And everyone's role in the company's success matters. If you're on the
front line, you're in the trenches and connected. You're the one leading the team huddles, rallying the troops, pulling people together,
and honoring best practices and routines. If everyone doesn't genuinely believe that what they do matters, neither will the customer or
anyone your organization interacts with. If everyone is empowered,
you will see and feel the difference. If the leaders are cared for, they
will pass that along.

Again, organizational culture isn't so different from firefighter culture. It's about a feeling. It's about respect. And it's about care+—your

leaders' care for their team members, upper management's care for their leaders, everyone's care for the mission and the purpose, and everyone's care for each other, including your guests. That's leading with meaning in a culture of care+.

What are some ways that you can create a firefighter culture of care+ for your team?

- Can you institute team huddles, whether virtually or in-person?

- How can you empower your team and leaders with information? Sneak peeks? Recognition?

- How are you listening to your team's input and challenges to best practices? And reprioritizing practices or workflows accordingly?

- When and how are you checking in with your team on what's going on in their life and offering assistance as possible?

Demonstrating care is often simpler and easier than we initially think. And the rewards you will reap, both spiritually and in your organization, are immense.

A Learning Culture

Caring is intimately connected to another key value intrinsic to a healthy culture: growth. And by that, I mean not just organizational growth, but also your team members' personal and professional growth. They're all connected. As we learn and grow as individuals, we have more knowledge to contribute. And the more a culture enables and promotes learning and growth, the happier, more empowered, and more effective the team will be. Which all leads to better outcomes. A culture of continuous learning is one of the best ways I know to enable that growth.

I've often felt that my bosses' care for my personal and professional growth through learning is a big part of why I ended up staying at Target. As I mentioned earlier, when I first started out at Marshall Field's, I wanted to go back to graduate school. Fairly soon, I did just that. I attended graduate school at the University of Chicago in the evenings part time, and I worked full time. I had internship requirements that I'd do at night, but I'd still do my job during the day. I'd be working on the L (Chicago's elevated trains), toting my school papers and a change of clothes in those big green Marshall Field's shopping bags. Which could have been a nightmare if my work managers hadn't supported my quest to better myself. But they did. I felt really cared for.

Target continues to support their employees' education and growth. And now it's easier than ever. One female entrepreneur developed a company I love called Guild. Guild serves as an intermediary between companies, their employees, and educational institutions, helping facilitate tuition-free education benefits for all. Participating employees can Dream to Be, whether that means finally getting their high school GED or an advanced degree, while companies can affordably help foot the bill. I know not every organization may be large enough to support their employees' entire education, but it's worth thinking about how you can support your team members' growth through learning, whether you're bolstering their educational goals financially or in other ways.

I still remember how John C., my manager at Marshall Field's, wanted me to be the community captain in our store. And no, it wasn't because no one else wanted it or because he wanted me out of his hair—it was because he saw the passion in me. He cared and he wanted to foster my growth. He saw I was bright and eager, and he was the kind of manager who knew that I needed to be nurtured. And he saw that I'd found my purpose in community.

"Here are some meaningful things you can do," he said to me one day as he handed me a binder.

He'd also anticipated my next question.

"And that department you're always asking about? Community Relations? Well, there's only two people in that area: the person who runs it and that person's assistant. So there aren't any openings—at least not yet. But check out the binder. It's got some things you can get started on immediately."

I checked out the binder. And got started on the various suggestions for getting involved in the community. And you know what? Two years later, John C. called.

"Remember that department of two? Well, one of those two people is hiring. And guess who is going to interview for the position? We have you in as a qualified applicant."

It wasn't a guarantee I would get the gig. But I was getting the interview! I was so excited I dropped my plans and spent the rest of the weekend studying up for the big meeting.

And yes, dear reader, I got the role: my very first job as a manager in community relations. It was 1993. Two years before, I'd been in Better Sportswear. Now I was a manager in a part of the business that was a perfect fit for my purpose. Remember Kassie? The woman who'd narrated the community relations video in my early days at

Marshall Field's? Well, it was Kassie, Kassie's assistant, and me. That's when I moved from the Water Tower Place store down to the inimitable State Street Marshall Field's. All because John C. cared and invested in my growth. It was just the beginning, but what a beginning it was. And the company's investment in me paid off as I in return invested in them. All because my manager had created a culture of learning and growth.

As the John C. story suggests, learning doesn't necessarily need to entail a formal degree. Education is continuous. But training is something your team benefits from and that, ideally, you're always providing. A culture of growth is a culture of continuous learning.

Remember our firefighters? Firefighters go through lots of training and upskilling. In some firehouses, there are classrooms for training with regular periodic workshops. Some of the training is also on the rigs. And some is community-based. Firefighters go everywhere from schools to senior homes to help community members prepare for what to do in case of emergency. They are not only the recipients of continuous training; they provide safety training to the community on a regular basis.

And let's not forget that most training and learning is on the job. There's a 70-20-10 rule that says 70 percent of our learning comes from challenging experiences on the job, 20 percent comes from developmental relationships, which we've covered extensively in this book, and 10 percent is coursework and training. So as a leader it's important to consider whether as part of the creation of a culture of learning you are providing new assignments for your team and keeping them continuously challenged and learning. As a leader who's leading with meaning you are always trying to champion the impact of others, a muscle they will strengthen as they continue their education.

Remember, we all contribute to an organization's culture of learning.

- If you're not in a position of leadership: If you have ideas for educational workshops or topics you'd like to learn more about, are you proposing them to leaders and/or participating in organizing them? Which outside speakers or experts might you want to suggest?

- If you're a leader: How can you help ensure your employees are continuously learning, upskilling, reskilling? What other support can you provide your employees to further their education besides financial support? Are there ways you can help people learn more on the job or ensure that they are getting challenging experiences and assignments?

A Culture of Trust

If you are leading with meaning, the third leg of the culture you're building is trust. Trust is the bedrock of high-performing teams.

We've already discussed building trust in several places in the book: through genuine listening and vulnerability in our relationships, as I learned with Dr. Lomax; through co-creation and mutual respect, as with my New York Crew; or simply through mentoring and challenging, as Michael Hyter did with me when he trusted me to move past my steak faux pas. Here I'd like to discuss other important elements in building trust. These include aligning your words with actions, demonstrating expertise, and building relationships through transparency and clarity. This trust framework is informed by research from Zenger Folkman, a global leadership development firm.

Our reputations are built not just on what we say but what we do. You often hear the saying that actions speak louder than words. For me that means you must follow through. "Execution, execution, execution" is one of my favorite mantras at work. The perception of us as trustworthy or not often depends on how aligned our actions are with our words.

Trust is also enhanced when you have demonstrated expertise in your role. Building your skills and being able to show others that you are equipped to do what you say you are going to do builds others' confidence in you. Having a subject matter skill, such as a demonstrated expertise in technology or accounting, makes you not just a valuable addition to any team but a trusted one. It frees everyone up to concentrate on where they are most needed when they know they belong to a team where everyone has their own special set of skills and can be trusted to execute their own piece of any project.

Finally, clarity and transparency help build trust. People want to know where they stand, what the central vision is, and what their individual goals are. A breakdown in trust—and transparency—often starts with confusion and a lack of clarity. Or as I often say, trust is clarity.

Again, firefighter culture is illuminating on this point. When you fight fires, you know what you're signing up for. Everyone knows their work is an opportunity to do an incredible service. They also all know the risks and rewards. And that any careless action can put them in harm's way. That after a trip out, every piece of gear must be stowed back in its proper place, as when that bell goes off, you're out the door and there's no time to go back and check if someone returned a crucial piece of equipment properly. That communication and assessment on the scene before jumping in is an imperative. What if it's a building where chemicals have been stored in a basement?

That dramatically changes the firefighting scenario, and everyone needs to communicate well and transparently up front about what they've discovered.

It's a similar situation in business. Transparency breeds trust and trust breeds transparency. And this goes for everything from individual feedback to much larger business decisions, such as reorganizations and corporate transitions.

When you give feedback, you need to be transparent or you will lose trust. You never want to make a person feel small or unvalued. But you may need to err on the uncomfortable side and get transparent with people when issues are cropping up. Ultimately, it will make people trust you more, not less, if you are honest with them.

One of our most stellar employees at Target was a guy I'll call Jimmy. Yet he wasn't always appreciated as such. Jimmy had a consulting background. He was so buttoned up that he had trouble connecting with people. The perception of Jimmy was that he was rigid. People wondered if he was truly listening to them or understood what they were saying. Like the Men in Black in the movies, Jimmy led with his IQ, not his EQ (emotional quotient). One of our leaders found it so frustrating, they tried to minimize his role and influence.

"He just isn't a team player," they'd say.

No one wanted to say anything directly to Jimmy. They didn't see the point. They didn't believe he could open up. Jimmy was about to get kicked off the island. He was simply seen as too tight.

Interestingly, I saw myself in Jimmy. I knew how it felt to keep things in. To try and focus on delivering and doing an exceptional job because you don't feel comfortable in other ways. It can be a way to compartmentalize and cope with your differences. You may not feel like you totally fit in, especially when you're new to an organization that was as large and complex as ours. So you try to show others that you're really good and capable, and can deliver results.

I also saw greatness in Jimmy. But I knew I had to be transparent with him about what was going wrong, or he wouldn't stand a chance. I felt like he had to spend less time proving himself to others and more time on himself. He had to loosen up and try to open up and connect. He wasn't my direct report, but I had spent time interviewing him and knew he was worth my efforts.

Luckily, I think Jimmy knew my intentions were good. I didn't sugarcoat it, but I also communicated that support. I told him what I was hearing from others. And I told him I was there to help to the extent I could, and I wanted him to be aware.

It was the push he needed.

He had to come to it in his own way, of course. For example, I was a hugger back then and still am. Jimmy would roll his eyes at my demonstrativeness. But in his own way, as he felt the trust I had for him, he in turn came to be more open, more transparent, and more trusting with me—and others. He is excelling. As he got comfortable in his own skin, he would even share pieces of his own story unprompted. All the things I'd seen in him were things I'd seen in myself. And his journey in a way became my journey too. I am so proud of him.

Now he's in the right role. He's soaring. And, in comparison to where he was, he *did* open up. All it took was some trust—and transparency. You can't evolve if you don't get constructive feedback. And you can't trust if you aren't trusted—and clearly shown the path.

Transparency, of course, is tricky when it comes to larger business issues like corporate restructurings or even unexpected events like the pandemic. I've often found it useful to make a distinction between clarity versus certainty. As a leader, you are always striving to be clear. Even when you can't always offer certainty.

When layoffs were absolutely necessary for the business, the goal was always to provide clarity about why we were doing them and what the company's priorities were. That kind of clarity is ground-zero-essential when you're entering a difficult or uncertain period. It's what enables people you hope will stick around to maintain their trust in you. We always tried to lay out where we were headed, acknowledge that it hurts, and maintain caring and clarity around the *why* of what we were doing.

What we couldn't do, of course, is offer complete certainty. You can't communicate certainty if you don't know more or can't say it. But you can be clear. And communicate as much as you know.

It also can be—and often must be—an evolving conversation. Because you often don't know what's coming down the pike. You only know what you've communicated. I've had people express to me in frustration, "Why didn't you tell me that six months ago?" I didn't know! I genuinely had been communicating what I knew at the time. Again, I was clear, but I wasn't certain.

And that philosophy changed how we prepped the leaders. We used to always say, "There are no more layoffs currently planned." But of course, there came a point where it was nearly impossible to say that with certainty. Instead, we'd say, and it was always true, "You can expect that we will regularly evaluate our cost structure and make ongoing changes to how we operate." It's about clarity. You've got to say what you mean, especially in times of uncertainty. And though you can't promise certainty, you can deliver clarity. Clarity, aligning your actions with your words, conveying your demonstrable expertise, and transparency are part of the culture of trust you're trying to create when you're leading with meaning.

Think of a situation you're in right now that requires trust.

- How are your actions aligning with your words?
- How are you effectively conveying your expertise?
- How can you be as clear as possible about what's happening or needed?
- How can you best phrase what you say to offer clarity without certainty?
- How can you offer support without certainty?

Practice how to support and be clear without sugar-coating or offering certainty. It's one of your most valuable leadership skills. And necessary for fostering trust.

I was lucky to spend decades at a corporation like Target whose motto eventually evolved from "Fast, Fun & Friendly" to "Care, Grow, and Win Together." If you see Target's values reflected in my own, it's only a sign of just how much it was both a top-down- but also bottom-up-guided culture. At Target, I lived through too many changes to enumerate—from changing the corporate name from Dayton-Hudson to Target, to restructurings, to the introduction of social media. But despite all the flux, a good culture can help sustain an organization and team through times of rapid change, adjustment, and even difficulty.

And as we look ahead and the world only moves faster and faster, I can't think of a more important lesson in leading with meaning than this one. Instilling and nurturing care+, learning, and trust in your people means that your people will always be able to roll with it and will continue to demonstrate care+, learning, and trust in return.

If you nurture the culture, you are cultivating the kind of mutual supportiveness, the kind that gave me chills, as I saw with the firefighters. You are nurturing people who will be there for each other— and you for them and they for you—even if you aren't spending all your time together or bunking together in the firehouse. You are creating a community that can sustain itself—through anything.

PS from Laysha

Creating and sustaining a culture of care+, learning, and trust is not just good for the team; it's good for business and organizational growth. With a strong foundation built on shared purpose and values, and sound strategy and processes, the team that cares about each other will always be more engaged, resilient, and successful.

CHAPTER NINE

Flourish Together

Seize the moments of happiness, love
and be loved! That is the only reality
in the world, all else is folly.

—LEO TOLSTOY

I t's lonely at the top."
     "Leadership is isolating."
     "You must take the road less traveled."
   We hear these mantras often. Perhaps we even readily accept the cliché that leadership is by its very nature a solitary job. The idea that the innovators, the leaders, the pioneers must go it alone is carved deep in the American psyche. As you've probably figured out by now, I beg to differ.

   I believe that it is relationships, not go-it-aloneness, that make a great leader. Soft skills are the new hard skills, and your ability to build relationships is critical to your business success. But building relationships with people you can count on matters beyond finding a circle of trustworthy advisors and building a great team and culture at work. Ideally, your circles of influence also include individuals who lift you up and hold your space. And those individuals aren't always in the workplace.

You need to create and sustain a personal life that will be there for you beyond the job. If you're lucky, you'll find great joy in your work, but few on their deathbed are thinking solely about their career accomplishments. You don't want to miss out on the joy of family, friends, and close relationships that will ultimately be your love letter to life.

Having those individuals in your life requires that you create space for them too. It requires you to make time to be there for others, and we all know time is a precious resource. And sometimes we feel so overwhelmed by career demands, especially when we are trying to lead with meaning, that we feel we have no room to support or further our more personal goals and needs. However, it's worth it. Family, found family, and partners fulfill us, uplift us, and help us reconnect with ourselves. Personal relationships can help you achieve your purpose and make an impact in ways that surpass what you could do without them.

When we are leading with meaning, we are trying to do fulfilling, often challenging things. But we don't have to do them alone.

Family You're Born Into and Family You Make

It may sound strange to talk about the importance of family support in a book on leadership. But as we've discussed, I believe that life and leadership are inextricably linked. You cannot flourish in one without flourishing in the other. And family is important. Whether you are close with your actual blood relations or with your found family, making time for them is making time for the kind of nurturance, uplift, and reconnection to our purpose we require if we want to lead with meaning.

The family you're born into and/or the family you make are the people who support you and whom you support in turn. Together you create a space where you can demonstrate the courage to be vulnerable. We need people who truly see us and whom we truly see. For it is by accessing our deepest vulnerabilities and desires together with those deeply trusted folks that we refill the well of inspiration and meaning.

My sister, Laynita (Nita), has been a crucial figure in my life. She's supported me and taught me much about living with integrity and love. She modeled for me *how* to follow my purpose. I remember watching her walk onto the Greyhound bus in Richmond, Indiana, the day she left home for Army boot camp. Her diminutive frame (she's smaller boned than I am) looked so out of place all alone on that bus. She was crying, I was sobbing, and our parents were trying to put on brave faces. It was hard watching her leave home. The Army hadn't been Nita's first choice, but she was proud to serve her country while also serving herself and our family. Nothing but nothing was more important to my parents than our education, and this way she would earn money and attend college in time. Maybe not the path she expected, but a path of perseverance and resilience that would eventually serve her needs and would serve as an example for me.

Nita served in the Army at Fort Hood (now called Fort Cavazos), Texas, for four years, and following active duty she was in the reserves for eight years. She ultimately attended Indiana University (IU), earning a merchandising degree. Today, she runs a successful IT consulting firm with her husband, Patrick. And she has used every single skill she developed in the Army and at IU. She fulfilled her purpose through hard work and determination, and as I watched and supported her taking every step, I promised myself I would work just as hard and be just as determined.

And thanks to Nita, I did and I was. I cobbled together enough funds to get to college through scholarships, loans, and multiple jobs. They certainly didn't cover everything—and every new semester was a question mark. But Nita was there for me all along the way, showing me what it looks like to persevere in the face of life's harsh realities. My purpose and work ethic, while duly influenced by my parents, were elevated and solidified by my big sis. She showed me that following your purpose is doing what you can with what you've got from where you are. She demonstrated for me what it means to nurture and display resilience, and always treated me with kindness and grace. I've tried to be supportive to Nita, though I'm not sure I was ever able to give back as much as I received from her. That said, I've always tried to pass on to others the love she's shown me.

Having a family member like Nita in your life is often a matter of luck. Nita is a blessing I couldn't consciously conjure for anyone else. But finding the individuals you can be truly close with also often comes from remembering to carve out the time in your life to share and return love, whether with good friends, family, or family figures. Love spreads, and the more you put out there, the more you attract in return.

Family you're born into can be an incredible anchor, especially when you are feeling like you've lost the path to fulfilling your purpose. But sometimes you need to look far outside your family—found or blood—and even far outside your workplace, to find a place where you can be truly yourself on a regular basis and stay connected to what you truly want. Sometimes you need to seek out new safe spaces and bonds. Which is how I found one of my most trusted relationships, Ms. Ruby.

When I moved to Minneapolis from Chicago, I had a whole lot of adjusting to do as a Black woman. From the start, I focused on building my professional skills and connections so I could be successful in my role and have an impact on the company and in the community. But I was struggling on the personal side of things. I was excelling at the work, but I didn't feel like I fit in. This was years before Mrs. King told me that corporate America could be my lunch counter, and I was beginning to question whether the Twin Cities was the right place for me. I was also working way too much to really figure out how to find my place in a new city. And I was still in graduate school at the University of Chicago when I made the move, periodically commuting back for lectures and classwork.

Being consumed by work isn't uncommon, especially at specific stages of our lives. There are periods where we are prioritizing our work and career. But doing so at the exclusion of any kind of personal life can have consequences.

I didn't know how badly I needed community and a space where I could fully be myself and fully support others until I found Ms. Ruby.

While beauty salons and barbershops are cornerstones of the Black community, most Black women are familiar with the challenges I faced in finding a good hairstylist (not to mention the lifelong frustration of spending hours on end in a salon). Initially it was a struggle to find somebody in Minneapolis who could not just do my hair, but who would have the right spirit and vibe and be flexible with my schedule.

Eventually I found a wonderful stylist, Ms. Ruby. At my very first appointment, the salon was full of stylists and customers—you could both feel and hear the energy. And yet amidst all of that buzz, when I met Ms. Ruby and sat down in her chair, I felt like I was the center of her attention. She asked questions to get to know me before we even talked about my hair. She had a big warm smile and the hours flew by.

From that day on, each time I sat in Ms. Ruby's chair, in addition to getting my hair done, I found community, connection, and solace. I began to feel more connected to the Twin Cities and Minnesota. And when I dropped into Ms. Ruby's chair, I could finally breathe.

I'm not exaggerating when I say that discovering Ms. Ruby has felt like a divine gift of sorts. Every time I sit in her chair, a part of me clicks into place. We listen to gospel and R&B music together, and we laugh and cry and pray together. Over the years, she has helped me piece myself together in ways that allowed me to not just survive but thrive. She provided a sense of home that helped bolster me whenever I was struggling. And she reminded me of my purpose, and of all the people I knew I wanted to be of service to, whenever that purpose felt adrift or misplaced.

I've tried to give back and support her in turn. I've followed her to every salon she's been part of and have been on a journey with her in every part of her personal and professional life. Throughout life's highs and lows, including a devastating tornado that tore through her neighborhood, we've been there for each other.

Found family doesn't have to be your hairstylist, of course. But I tell you this story to show how finding support and camaraderie often happens in the most unexpected ways and in the most unexpected places. I encourage you to lean in to these unanticipated encounters. I found Ms. Ruby by being open to the possibility of our relationship being something more than transactional. And in my being open to her, she found me.

Your personal life matters, and staying connected to your family and found family will help sustain you, create a space of love and uplift, and keep you connected to your purpose. Here are some questions to ask yourself, especially when work is taking over your life:

- Who inside or outside of your immediate family shows up for you and helps you survive and thrive?

- Who do you give that support to?

- When was the last time you reached out to them, whether they're family you were born with or family you've made?

- Did you make it a point to talk about something truly meaningful to both of you?

- What did you learn about each other? Did it help you reaffirm your purpose and theirs?

Reach out this week.

Resilience and Love Matter

A life partner is a choice. To be clear, I don't think you have to have a partner. But if you choose to have one, and I did, the choice matters. It needs to be a mutually supportive relationship, not one that will be at odds with your desire to lead the life you're meant to lead.

The ultimate goal is to find someone with whom you have a shared commitment, and who is willing and able to work with you through the vicissitudes of life. Your ability to work through complex choices together at home parallels your ability to work through difficult choices in *all* aspects of your life. By working through complexity, not being paralyzed by it, you will find satisfaction and joy in the outcome. Doing that with someone else lightens the load.

Which is why, hopefully, whether you have a partner or not, you'll find some lessons in my story about finding resilience, forgiveness, and, yes, even love. Resilience is a trait that helps us work through the complexity. Forgiveness, love, and acting with integrity and humanity—these are the core values of leading with meaning. Whether love is in your life with a partner or in other ways, embracing love and joy is crucial to your personal fulfillment and flourishing.

Committing to a partner is a very personal decision. And it's often complicated. Everyone is going to have a different constellation of forces and factors they work through. Every choice is an individual one. But I encourage you to keep going if the person merits it. If they don't, you have another choice to make. But if they do, there is something good on the other side. You don't want to miss out on what's meant for you.

Something else I've learned along the way: You will need to make space for and work on this relationship, like all important personal relationships, if you want to sustain your holistic approach to your life and career journey. As with any important relationship, you need to make time to ensure you're growing together rather than apart. Along the way, you will face challenges that you'll need to work through together and overcome.

My husband, Bill Kiffmeyer, is my ultimate partner in life. Being married to Bill has wholly transformed my life, making it easier for me to live in service to my purpose. Bill is a little kid in a sixty-year-old's body. Anyone who knows him well would say that he has a childlike, joyful spirit. Despite one of his common refrains—"I don't work for you"—he shows up for me in endless ways, at work, at home, and in the community.

But before I dive into the very personal story of my marriage, I want to highlight a different marriage between two people I know who set an incredible example for Bill and me over the years—the late General Colin Powell and Alma Powell. I always saw a deep level of respect and admiration when they spoke to one another. One never knows what another marriage looks like from the inside, but for all intents and purposes, theirs seemed to be a model of mutual support and trust of the kind that enables purpose to flourish. I saw their humanity with each other and picked up on important lessons for my own marriage.

It was empowering for me to see how Alma Powell fulfilled her role as General Powell's equal partner. While she proudly supported her husband's military career, she also served as the chair of the board of directors for America's Promise, wrote several children's books, and was on an advisory board to support historically Black colleges and universities with President Barack Obama. Although General Powell held powerful titles throughout his military career, in the Powell household he always made sure that others knew that he and Alma were co-generals.

I recently ran across one of my favorite pictures of the Powells where Alma is standing at a podium and General Powell is sitting nearby, beaming with pride. You could tell that he was reveling in the joy of sitting back and watching her run the show. I'm honored that I got to witness these two incredible people shine the light on each other, showing the rest of us what is possible when you are committed to the growth and evolution of your life partner. The Powells broke out of typical societal norms for what a husband and wife should be and do for each other by defining and designing their marriage in a way that made sense for their family—transformational, grounded in purpose, and steeped in truth and love.

When Bill and I first started dating back in 1991, and then married in 1998, we had limited ideas about what a marriage could look like. But as our careers and lives began evolving in very different directions, suddenly the questions about how a marriage could and should work became more important and relevant. There is no way that I could have predicted that I would go from a sales associate to a C-suite executive. It's been an exciting ride, but it's also introduced some unexpected turns for both Bill and me.

Because of the nature of my work, I am often in the spotlight, which is very different from Bill, who has a PhD in anatomy and is a molecular biologist. I often call him my own mad scientist. Bill has had incredible success and impact in his career—but his success has looked different from mine. Over the years the differences between my highly visible corporate job and his behind-the-scenes science role have created some challenging dynamics between us.

I remember having a conversation with General Powell about this issue when my role was growing and my calendar was loaded down with events and travel. I shared with him that I was concerned that my career was starting to get in the way of my healthy marriage. Without hesitation, he said, "Then your number one priority is to make sure your career doesn't get in the way." Coming from Colin Powell it sounded so simple. But at the time, it was anything but simple.

Over time, Bill and I have created our own definition of what a successful partnership looks like for us. Like the Powells, we too have realized that neither one of us has to dim our light in order for the other to shine. I can now recognize how fortunate I was to find a partner willing to adjust to the reality of my unexpected career, pushing me further in the direction of my purpose and transforming my life.

Even though we eventually found our rhythm in balancing our careers and our marriage, we are no strangers to tough times in our relationship. And of all the stories about being the first, the only, or one of a few, this one is the hardest for me to tell.

Bill and I have an interracial marriage, one that would have been illegal in this country before 1967, when the landmark U.S. Supreme Court case *Loving v. Virginia* invalidated laws that prohibited people like Bill and me from being married and sharing a life. Thankfully, we were able to marry and our union has lasted for almost three decades.

Yet despite the harmony we've achieved together, we've also had to face some rather significant challenges from our careers and from inside our families. We've needed to develop our resilience as a result. And we've needed to find our own way to forgiveness and love.

Some of these challenges appeared in even our earliest days together. Bill comes from a big, rowdy German American family who couldn't accept that he wanted to marry a Black woman. They had never met me, yet they couldn't accept me based on the color of my skin. Not the greatest way to start a life together. When Bill and I were still dating, he would come to Chicago to visit me regularly. During one of his visits, we received a very upsetting phone call from his parents. Somehow Bill's parents had figured out who he was dating—and they tracked down my phone number. (There were no cell phones yet, so this was a landline call.) When they asked to speak with Bill, I gingerly handed the phone over to him. I watched as Bill's face fell as he listened to them telling him that he was going to ruin his life if he continued to date me. We heard every horrible stereotype imaginable.

It is difficult to put into words what that moment felt like for me and what it must have felt like for Bill. I was having an out-of-body experience that left me deeply shaken, rattled, and pissed off. I knew Bill was deeply wounded, but he didn't pack up his bags and leave. It was my first inkling that no matter what, we would figure out a way to be each other's harbor in any storm we encountered.

Thankfully, Bill's siblings stood by us from the beginning of our relationship. But even after we got married and were finding our rhythm as a couple, the early wounds from not being accepted as an interracial couple had not fully healed.

As we continued to deal with all that, our work-life complexities were also driving a wedge between us that we just couldn't seem to work our way out of. We had moved to Minneapolis for my job. We often found ourselves on different trajectories, both traveling a lot for work. We were sometimes two ships passing in the night. What most people around us didn't know is that we separated for a while.

I sometimes wondered if we were giving up too much in loving each other. I was worried I was "selling out." My purpose is to be of service to others, especially to women, people of color, and other underrepresented communities. But here I was, being rejected for my skin color. All of this was happening as I was searching for my place in corporate America and the world. Sometimes, when I look back, I'm surprised I even made it out the door in the morning. But I did. Armor on, ready to face the day on the outside—while dying a little on the inside.

While we were separated and moving toward a divorce, I was still working, traveling, and doing everything to show up at work as best as I could. But for many days during that time, I was a hot effing mess. I lost fifteen pounds and was the skinniest that I'd ever been in my adult life. The people around me had no idea that this was how I was feeling. I was silently suffering because I didn't feel in a position to ask for help. I don't have many regrets, but not asking for help during that time is one of them.

Just as Bill and I were getting ready for mediation and preparing to move forward with a divorce, we did the hard work to come back from the brink. With the help and support of other people we trusted in our lives, including a spiritual counselor and a therapist, we learned to recognize the value in ourselves and in each other. What we took away from the process of working through our difficulties reinforces for me why Bill was and continues to be my partner in life. Bill would often say, "If we are going to make it, you have to forgive yourself, and you have to forgive me." This was the truth that I needed to hear over and over again—and put into practice.

I now knew I had his support to show up as exactly who I am, as someone who works a lot, as someone who travels a lot, and, of course, as a Black woman. And knowing his support was unconditional meant I could return it in turn. We could show up as exactly who we both were—as individuals and as a couple.

I came to realize, through time and a mix of joy and pain, that when you're holding on to grudges, your hands aren't free to catch blessings. I had to be willing to forgive. While I would never be able to forget some of the difficult times, to keep Bill in my life—and for my own sanity—I had to find grace. Eventually, all of us, including the members of his family, discovered that there was someone we loved more than we hated our differences—and that someone was Bill. I am so thankful that we all got to that point where our family dynamic is driven by love and forgiveness rather than a deep divide.

I've never talked about our marriage this openly before, and it's still very challenging and emotional at times. But I want our story to be of service to others. At the end of the day, my marriage with Bill and the Powells' marriage aren't fairy tales about a prince and a princess falling in love and living happily ever after. Every marriage has its lions, tigers, and bears too.

We are still a work in progress.

When your spouse is a genuine partner, and you are devoted to

204 LEAD LIKE YOU MEAN IT

each other, you help each other stay true to what you are called to do. Even through those difficult times, Bill didn't waver in supporting me in my personal and professional purpose. And I didn't waver in supporting him. We always made it a priority to discuss and wrestle with the challenges that were pulling us apart. Ultimately, we found joy, hope, and love amidst the struggle. We found a way to flourish together.

Working through complex challenges in our relationships requires—and even strengthens—our resilience. I hope you've found some comfort and hope in my story, whether you have a partner or not. I do believe that at some point all of us have reasons to choose love and forgiveness. And the result is joy and mutual fulfillment.

- How can you support those you are in close relationships with?

- How can they support you and your purpose? How can you both make sure your lights are never dimmed?

- If this isn't a conversation you've ever had with your partner or others, try it.

PS from Laysha

We all need to be nourished in order to flourish. We are not made to fly solo through the stages of our life or career. As the fabulous Maya Angelou said, it may in fact be utterly impossible to be successful without helping others be successful. We all flourish together. Amen.

Benediction

W hen I look back on my childhood, I will always fondly remember the fellowship I enjoyed at church, where the pastors and elders would stand strong and always be ready with an encouraging word.

At the end of every good church service, the pastor leaves the worshippers with a benediction to reinforce the lessons from the morning sermon and bless them forward to carry what they have learned into the world. In this benediction, while I'm certainly not a pastor, I will leave you with a few final thoughts on how to lead like you mean it to carry you through your life and leadership learning journey.

But first, a story.

When I was about four or five years old, we lived in a little house in Richmond, Indiana. Richmond was small, yet significantly bigger than Fountain City, where I spent most of my formative years. Richmond was predominantly a manufacturing town, in my memory, known for two local businesses in particular: Tom Raper RVs and Pizza King. It also had a history of recording jazz musicians, including many of the greats, such as Louis Armstrong and Jelly Roll Morton. With a population of about forty thousand, Richmond had a tiny Main Street, a department store, and a lot of mom-and-pop establishments.

A lot of families have their holiday traditions. One of ours was to make a list of everything we wanted for Christmas. We never got everything on our Christmas list, and we knew we couldn't put big-ticket items on it anyway. But my parents always did their best to make sure that we got at least something we really wanted and that there were presents under the tree.

While living in Richmond, we had an extra tradition on Christmas Eve. My parents would place under the tree three or four small packages each for me, my sister, Nita, and my brother, Eric. We knew we'd be getting more presents the next day. These were like the pregame—we were getting excited for the big event.

My mother, Gloria, was the mastermind behind this tradition, and Dad went along and fully supported it. My parents would talk to us about how though they were working hard, and we didn't have a lot of money, there were even less fortunate people who had less than we did. And it was important for us to help other people. This isn't to say that we didn't ever need help, but for my parents this was a lesson in generosity and paying it forward. And in a season that often became all about what people wanted, and could get, they were teaching us how to give and be of service to others. They were teaching us how to lead with meaning.

The three or four gifts were wrapped, so you didn't know what was inside. We were asked to select one of those items, still wrapped, that had been on our Christmas list, and give it away to a child who was the same age as us. We did later get to open the other small packages. But the first order of things was to give something away. We'd meet the children we were giving the gifts to in person; sometimes they were even just an alley away. This wasn't faceless giving. It was recognizing the individuals around us and their humanity. It was being of service to people in our community, whether you knew them or not.

When I reflect on the lessons I've tried to impart in this book about how we can lead with meaning, I often think back to this foundational lesson from my childhood. At that age it was a lot to process. I was giving up something that I wanted and that meant something to me. But what I realized over time was that my parents were right: The joy was in the giving as much as the getting. And that's a key lesson I hope to leave you with.

♠

Leading with meaning is acting with integrity and humanity. It's forging relationships with many different kinds of people, from many different walks of life. And it's about being of service, even while pursuing the goal of growth and flourishing—for you, your organization, and your community. It's about taking a holistic approach to your life and career and always being in service to your purpose. It's about leaving things and people better off than you found them. It's about sustaining and championing others and leaving a legacy of leadership.

Finding your why or your purpose will help you achieve things that seem impossible. That's the kind of radical growth you can experience when you're willing to open yourself up to the transformative power of knowing your purpose in life.

Opening yourself up to finding relationships in all walks of life will help you achieve your purpose. By challenging our assumptions, celebrating our wins, and comforting us in defeat, our most meaningful relationships keep us moving forward in the direction of our purpose. I have always appreciated the gold that I mined from my foundational support system, my parents, Gloria and Eugene. Whether your family is found or blood relations, we gain strength and resilience from one another and within each other find the encouragement to lead a meaningful life.

Leading with meaning pushes us to claim our own space while making room for others to claim theirs. As we pursue our purpose and co-create, we also champion others to have an impact. We add more seats at the table, create our own tables, break glass ceilings, and send the elevator of success back down for others.

I've shared some painful and joyful moments in this book, but I want to close on a note of joy because I am filled with gratitude for the multitude of life and leadership lessons the people I've come to know through my quest to be of service have bestowed on me. They made it possible for me to forge a path that is uniquely mine. I have tried to pass on their many lessons and create possibilities for others.

Now it's time to step passionately into your purpose and into a world that needs you. Onward.

Lead Like You Mean It Anthem

You are a fundamental part of my story,
Dare I say a quintessential part of my love letter to life.
You believed in me before I believed in myself.
You are a rock,
Who urged me to stand in my power and purpose.
And I do until I can't.
Then you say, "I am your rock, lean on me,"

And I flow between resilience and rest.

Dammit I need to rest.

Yet I'm still joyful, hopeful.

Life is for the livin' amidst its vicissitudes,

And so I march,

As did my ancestors,

Onward.

Stepping into and onto stones toward life and light,

My fear and flight through what was and what is,

Into my birthright,

A calling that is divinely mine for the taking.

Mine.

Ours.

To be shared and given to the world.

So from my lunch counter a change is gonna come.

I'ma keep on steppin' till it's done.

And will be there to support and advocate for you

As you step into your own.

Acknowledgments

With Deepest Gratitude

Every day, I practice a gratitude ritual where I identify three things I am grateful for. Inspired by Shawn Achor, a friend and noted happiness expert, this practice makes me happy and reminds me, even on my worst days, that I am fortunate to be living this life.

Writing my first book afforded me the opportunity to learn and grow in unexpected new ways. It was a workout like nothing I've ever experienced! It was humbling, motivating, frustrating, and rewarding all at once. I built some new muscles and stamina through the process, and I'm stronger as a result.

The magic in the madness of this years-long process was conjured by the community of wise and wonderful people who gave their time, talent, and treasures to this book. They understood and honored my dream of capturing shared stories around a shared table of life and leadership.

I want to acknowledge the individuals who made space for me and this passion project. We all walk a unique path, but we are interconnected. And I am truly grateful for each of you.

First, a note of love and gratitude to my parents—my mom, Gloria, and my late father, Gene, who together instilled in me the importance of serving others, faith, family, learning, and doing my best. I was raised by a pair of O.G. book hoarders, so I know they're proud that I am now an author. There will be a signed copy of my book in heaven for you, Dad.

To my ride-or-die husband, best friend, and rock, Bill Kiffmeyer. I can't imagine going through this thing called life with anyone other than you. The pages of this book and the chapters of my life have your imprint all over them. Love you.

And to the constellation of stars in my book-writing universe, without whom I wouldn't have been able to write or publish this book: You lit the way at every turn.

First, Kari Thompson of 44 Degrees North Partners, who has been on this wild ride with me from the very beginning. You have been chief of staff, strategist, dreamer, believer, and doer. You invested in me and this project like it was your very own in ways that have been game-changing for me. Thank you for bringing your big brain and big heart to this work. You are a sister friend. I see you and you see me.

Cheers!

To Peter Steinberg, my literary agent at United Talent Agency, thanks for the guidance and support you gave this first-time author who knew very little about what I was getting into. You showed me the ropes of writing my first book proposal, developing a clear pitch to publishers, assembling a team of collaborators, and so much more. What an education.

Sometimes the universe brings you full circle. I couldn't have imagined that my book would be published by The Open Field, a publishing imprint by Maria Shriver and Penguin Random House. I met the inimitable Maria, a true force for good in the world, more than twenty years ago when we joined forces to support the Women's Conference in California, which she was leading at the time. Maria, you are an architect of change and a remarkable woman of courage, wisdom, strength, and faith. I'm blessed that you continue to encourage me to take bold leaps of faith to make a difference.

I won the authors' lottery when Meg Leder became my editor extraordinaire. Meg, you have a gift, and I am forever grateful to be the beneficiary of your expertise. You pushed me and my team to keep the reader at the center of the work so that it met their needs and as such fulfilled my mission to make this book a resource that would help and inspire people on their journey. You and your team—including Isabelle Alexander, Shelby Meizlik, Anna Brill, and Bridget Gilleran—provided phenomenal and thoughtful and sometimes mind-twisting feedback. You showed that you cared. I appreciate you.

To my ghostwriter, Dedi Felman, the quintessential Book Doctor. You are gifted in the art and science of storytelling, which makes you a talented film and TV writer and director too. You ask probing questions, you push for the deeper lesson, and you are curious, creative, and determined. You made the book—and me—better. And you were right, the book reveals itself over time and throughout the ever-evolving process. Much like life. Girl, you, Kari, and I shared our lives over Zoom for the better part of a year. Thank you for challenging our corporate lingo and flexing with our unusual process. We did it!

A big shout-out to the extraordinary Matie Argiropoulos, executive producer, and team for your guidance, expertise, and care in helping me bring my audiobook to life! It was a whole vibe.

Behind the scenes, I was also blessed with first-rate leadership development counsel from my friend and former colleague Corey Criswell of Adeption. Corey, I am in awe of your ability to make leadership development accessible, practical, and fun. Thank you for sharing your knowledge and perspective.

To Eric Erickson of Erickson McGee, and Sarah McNerney, two of the best creatives I know, thank you for ideating with me at various points in the journey of this book and for bringing my brand to life.

Celebrating my sister friend, the fabulous Sharon Smith Akinsanya, owner of Rae Mackenzie Group, along with Kimberly Steward and team, for your strategic input and execution of my brand.

To Bill Tamlyn, my speechwriter for nearly twenty years, I hope you see yourself in these pages because many of the words you've written for me have become essential parts of my story. Thank you.

And to my unofficial Target/Dayton-Hudson historian and archivist Susan Kahn, founder of 44 Degrees North Partners, thank you for keeping me honest by validating certain details given I didn't have a written journal of my corporate stories, just my memories. Your robust collection of annual reports and keen editor's eye were invaluable assets in this process.

To Denver Gilliand and Klair Reese of DSG Capital Advisors, your wise and expert counsel and vast network of expert resources have ensured that I made informed and sound decisions at every step along the journey. Bill and I are glad you're on our team.

Thanks to Theresa "T" Nichols and her superb executive assistant skills. We kept all the disparate parts aligned and moving in harmony.

To Team Tarzhay—my bosses, peers, and teammates at Target over the decades—I hit the bullseye when I joined this special brand. At the close of my nearly thirty-three years, I extended my deepest affections and gratitude for all the lessons learned, the successes and challenges, the relationships, and the impact that allowed us to get better together. The best is yet to come and I'm confident you've got this!

To all the authors who gave me advice on writing and promoting a book, your generosity means everything to me, and I promise to pay it forward. In the words of one of those authors, the fabulous Pearl Cleage, I speak your names:

Arthur C. Brooks

Ursula Burns (Thanks to my friend and former peer at Target, Don Liu, for making this connection.)

Pearl Cleage

Carla Harris

Walter Isaacson

Luvvie Ajayi Jones

Debra Lee

Marisa Renee Lee

Indra Nooyi (Thanks to my former boss Brian Cornell for connecting me with Indra.)

Michele Norris

Reshma Saujani

Cleo Wade

I had an idea for a book percolating in my mind for more than a decade. It was not the book you are holding right now—but the concept informed and influenced *Lead Like You Mean It*. I envisioned a book called *Love Letters to Life*. I imagined asking people to contribute their own love letters to their lives as part of my story. I wanted to capture my deep appreciation for the limited, precious journey we are given on this earth. And I wanted to illustrate the power that can come from writing about what's most important to you in this life—while you are still alive. Ultimately, I wanted to inspire people to live, lead, and love fully, something I work on doing every day. Because when the journey ends, we all want to leave behind an extraordinary love letter to life to inspire those who will carry our legacies forward. Jim Hogan, Target colleague and friend, wrote his own love letter to life that he shared with me a couple of months before he passed away from cancer. Jim was a shining example of the power of human connection and the lasting legacy of authentic relationships.

It is in that spirit of authentic human connection that I give thanks to Joyce Melzer, our former landlord and my second mom from my Chicago days. I love watching you, in your eighties, continue to host and participate in your book club thanks to audiobooks. I read my audiobook in your honor.

To the enormous village of people throughout my life, some captured in this book, but many who aren't, I am blessed and highly favored for the many ways you have added to my life and leadership journey. The rest of my story, of our story, is still being written. And I am honored to travel this journey with you.

And lastly, to you, the reader: Thank you for picking up this book, for reading, and for joining my community at layshaward.com. We all have something to learn, and we all have something to teach. I look forward to connecting with you.